Up the Strait

Note for Librarians: a cataloguing record for this book that includes
Dewey Decimal Classification and U.S. Library of Congress numbers is
available from the Library and Archives of Canada. The complete
cataloguing record can be obtained from their online database at:
www.collectionscanada.ca/amicus/index-e.html

ISBN 978-0-9781357-2-0
Printing coordinated by Lulu.com, Raleigh, NC

Powell River Books

Pomona, CA, USA
Book sales online at:
www.powellriverbooks.com
phone: 604-483-1704
email: wlutz@mtsac.edu

· 10 9 8 7 6 5 4 3 2 1

Up the Strait

Coastal British Columbia Stories

Wayne J. Lutz

2007

Powell River Books

Other Books by Wayne J. Lutz

Up the Lake
Up the Main
Up the Winter Trail

To Jim...

Wharfinger of Powell River's Westview Harbour,
gateway to the Strait of Georgia.
Jim always finds a way to get it done.

The stories are true, and the characters are real.
Some details are adjusted to protect the guilty.
All of the mistakes rest solidly with the author.

Front Cover Photo:
Powell Lake, south of Second Narrows near Rainbow Lodge; Powell
Lake was an inlet of the Strait of Georgia until 10,000 years ago.
Back Cover Photos:
Top – Prideaux Haven, Desolation Sound
Bottom – Westview's North Harbour and Harwood Island

Acknowledgements

My editors assist me under very demanding conditions. I write fast, often without sufficient attention to the standards of good grammar. Quantity is never a problem in my writings – it's that quality thing that hangs over my head. As other authors are aware, writing is the easy part. It is the polish of editing that consumes the most effort.

Editing chapters as changes are incorporated into the manuscript is a gruelling process. Margy Lutz constantly reviewed these chapters, always improving my writing. For this book, Jena Lohrbach edited my writing for the first time. She brings a valuable background in publishing to the editing process. Samantha Macintyre again provided editing assistance, improving my writing techniques in the process.

Frank Mayne provided guidance for the Powell Lake deep water sample project that forms a theme for several chapters of this book. Frank, I'm pleased to report the Kemmerer bottle made it back to the surface from 1100 feet down.

The Maithi clan supports my writing in more ways than I can document here. My books are continually influenced by their contributions. Ed Maithus draws cartoons with the originality readers of this series have come to expect. John Maithus constantly teaches me about boats, Powell Lake, and the Strait of Georgia. When I run into trouble on the water, my first thought is: "What would John do in this situation?" It has bailed me out of a lot of challenging conditions.

Wayne J. Lutz
Powell Lake, BC
May 1, 2007

Contents

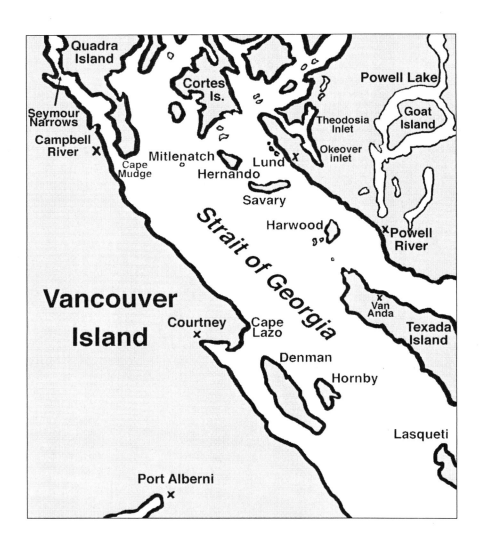

Quadra
Island

Cortes
Is.

Powell Lake

Seymour
Narrows

Theodosia
Inlet

Goat
Island

Campbell
River

Okeover
inlet

Mitlenatch

Lund

Cape
Mudge

Hernando

Savary

Harwood

Powell
River

Vancouver

Strait of Georgia

Van
Anda

Island

Courtney

Cape
Lazo

Texada
Island

Denman

Hornby

Lasqueti

Port Alberni

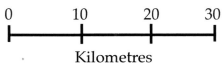

0   10   20   30

Kilometres

Lower Coastal
British Columbia

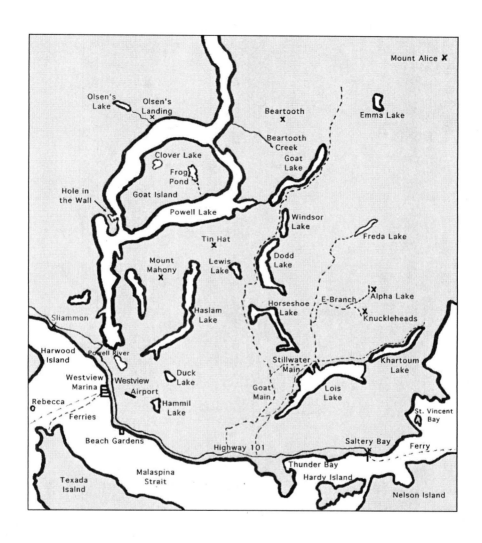

Mount Alice ✗

Olsen's Lake · Olsen's Landing ✗

Beartooth ✗

Emma Lake

Beartooth Creek

Clover Lake · Frog Pond

Goat Lake

Hole in the Wall · Goat Island

Powell Lake

Windsor Lake

Freda Lake

Tin Hat ✗

Mount Mahony ✗

Lewis Lake

Dodd Lake

E-Branch · Alpha Lake ✗

Horseshoe Lake

Sliammon

Haslam Lake

Knuckleheads ✗

Harwood Island · Powell River

Stillwater Main

Khartoum Lake

Westview Marina · Westview Airport

Duck Lake

Goat Main

Lois Lake

Rebecca

Hammil Lake

St. Vincent Bay

Ferries

Beach Gardens

Highway 101

Saltery Bay · Ferry

Texada Isalnd

Malaspina Strait

Thunder Bay · Hardy Island

Nelson Island

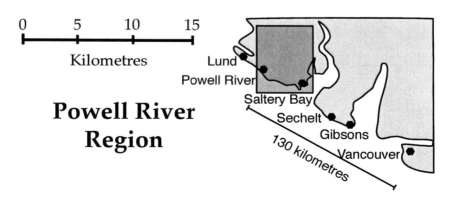

0   5   10   15
Kilometres

Lund
Powell River
Saltery Bay
Sechelt
Gibsons
Vancouver

130 kilometres

Powell River Region

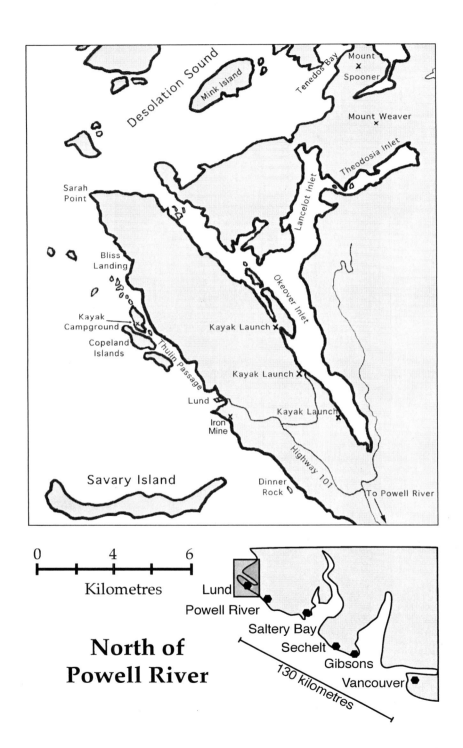

Desolation Sound

Mink Island

Tenedos Bay

Mount Spooner ×

Mount Weaver ×

Theodosia Inlet

Lancelot Inlet

Sarah Point

Okeover Inlet

Bliss Landing

Kayak Campground ×

Kayak Launch ×

Copeland Islands

Thulin Passage

Kayak Launch ×

Lund

Kayak Launch ×

Iron Mine ×

Savary Island

Dinner Rock

Highway 101

To Powell River

0   4   6

Kilometres

North of
Powell River

Lund

Powell River

Saltery Bay

Sechelt

Gibsons

Vancouver

130 kilometres

Preface

Sublime

"**I**'m okay now!" I yell above the noise of the motor.

The boat's canvas enclosure is buttoned up against the weather, but the windshield has not yet cleared from the moisture lingering inside. To allow some circulation, I have unzipped the small opening above the center windshield and tossed back the flap. Every time the Campion whacks into a wave, water splashes over the bow and into the opening. I receive a blast of water across my face every few seconds as we pound through the waves near Haywire Bay. But now I'm finally okay.

We left the Shinglemill only a few minutes ago, and I was grumpy. Loading the boat included shoving a giant cardboard box containing a futon into the stern, and then pushing it the front to balance awkwardly between the seats. The big box had to be jammed as far forward as possible to allow the rear canvas cover to snap into position, with little room remaining for Margy and me. Getting into the driver's position required climbing over the back of the seat and sliding clumsily into the captain's chair.

It's been a race against rain, which is still threatening. Out of sight on the other side of the cardboard box is Margy, being splashed by the waves as much as I am. She listened to my grumbling as we loaded the boat with the futon, six bags of groceries, two containers of gasoline, a bag of clean laundry, our backpacks, and three 8-litre containers of water. She hauled as many supplies from the truck as I did, and put up with my bad attitude every step of the way. She even tried to assist with the futon, but could do little more than help balance the box as I struggled with it. Margy knows this type of physical labor makes me grumpy and that the wisest course of action is to simply stay clear.

The water splashing through the open hatch is now making a mess out of the cardboard box, as well as drenching us both. But it beats trying to see through a fogged windshield. A loose yellow life vest flies over the box, dangling from Margy's hand.

"Thanks," I say. In my haste, I forgot to put on my life vest. Now I struggle with it in the cramped space between the box on one side and the hull-mounted throttle on the other. Driving this boat while putting on a life vest is difficult in the best of conditions. But now, for the first time this afternoon, I'm okay.

"Do you know why I'm finally okay?" I ask.

"Sure," replies Margy with certainty. "You're finally going up the lake."

It's amazing what this lake does to me.

"It makes all of the difference in the world," I proclaim.

"I've noticed."

My head and chest are drenched, the box with its valuable cargo is dripping wet, I'm sweating from the confined damp air in the boat, and dark clouds surround us in all directions. But the scenery is sublime. Wispy white stratus clouds hang low along the edge of the lake on all sides, in contrast to the higher gray layer that is about to pour down on us. The mountains along the shoreline jut nearly straight up from the lake, disappearing into the overcast.

I've gone from frustrated to serene in a matter of minutes, a sudden transformation that's difficult to justify. One thing for certain – it's because I'm traveling up the lake in a region whose beauty is difficult to describe. It's a lake that affects my entire being.

* * * * *

Sublime – of such excellence, grandeur, or beauty so as to inspire great admiration or awe; almost heavenly.

Sublime implies a quiet, peaceful encounter with majestic scenery, the kind of awe-inspiring vistas that make the Powell River region so magical. Sublime goes beyond beauty. Historian Jacques Barzun writes in *From Dawn to Decadence*, a history of the past 500 years: "Beauty is smooth and harmonious and agreeable. The sublime is rugged, outsized, and terrifying."

I've driven my boat up the lake to my cabin countless times. On each trip, I'm reminded of the scope of the sublime. Mountains with rich green forests rise from Powell Lake. Glaciated peaks provide a backdrop for towering firs and cedars. It grabs your attention, and reminds you of the relative lack of importance of life's day-to-day problems.

Similarly, a trip up the Strait of Georgia is an inspirational journey. Desolation Sound, at the strait's northern end, was named by famous navigator George Vancouver. This unlikely name for such a beautiful body of water was the result of one of the depressed moods that often haunted Vancouver during his important 1790s voyage to explore and chart the northwest coast of the Americas. Any who have seen this glorious maze of islands, headlands, and ocean inlets would be hard pressed to understand Vancouver's bouts of despondency. Even in the dreariest of weather, the mountains of Desolation Sound rise majestically from the sea. The panorama is beyond breathtaking.

Canadian authors, like Stephen Hume and Susanna Moodie, have documented the intense effect of Canadian landscapes on the soul. Hume recounts the experience of being alone in a remote area of the Northwest Territories: "What seemed desolate was rich and full." Take that, Vancouver.

Moodie writes of the "sublime solitude" of Canada's forests, equating encounters with the vast stands of trees to feeling the presence of God. It doesn't get more sublime than that.

Our concept of wilderness contributes to the awe we see in nature. The risks associated with remote areas grab us, sometimes shaking us to our senses. Eric Collier wrote in *Three Against the Wilderness*: "In the wilderness you seem to realize the omnipresence of danger." We go there, we sense the danger, and we bask in the pleasure of not being afraid. It is reassuringly sublime.

Canadians seem to take their country's majestic vistas for granted. But it's only an act. In *The Canadian Identity*, nature writer Fred Bodsworth notes: "There are more paintings of wilderness lakes, spruce bogs and pine trees on more Canadian living room walls than in any other nation on earth."

The feeling I get when exposed to majestic Canadian scenes can be equated to another experience I've enjoyed for decades – flying. I look down on the world from my Piper Arrow and realize how unimportant our daily worries are when seen from a spectacular airborne viewpoint.

Similarly, from the ground, remote landscapes put our lives into a different perspective. In *Off the Map*, Hume writes: "And that's one of the wonders you discover in wilderness: everything operates on a scale that makes your own life appear frenzied and even foolish."

Get in your boat and head up the Strait of Georgia. You'll encounter no uncertainties regarding its beauty. The Strait of Georgia is sublime.

◊ ◊ ◊ ◊ ◊ ◊ ◊

Chapter 1

So Near, Yet So Far

I roll down the hill from the airport in my old Ford Tempo, yellow banana (kayak) on top. The late afternoon sky is clear, and the Strait of Georgia is nearly calm. I can see all the way to Comox, with Mount Washington's cap of snow clearly visible on this warm September day.

In celebration of my arrival in Powell River, I continue all the way downhill to the wharf, where I can get an overall perspective of the chuck. Although it's a Sunday, maybe Jim's shop is open so I can get a few supplies. I need a tide book that extends farther north, and I'm looking for some teak varnish to seal the weathered wood on the aft deck of the Bayliner.

As I pass Marine Traders, there are few cars in the parking lot, but maybe Jim's shop is open today. I'll return to the store in a few minutes, but my focus is now on the wharf. The traffic light at the ferry terminal parking lot is red, so I stop. But after peering into the parking area, it's obvious the light has no meaning. Neither the Texada nor Comox ferry is docked. The ferry lot contains only a brown pickup truck and a yellow DHL van, so I slip through the red light and make the right turn into the sandy parking area. There isn't a designated parking lot, but I pull off to the side at a comfortable angle and stop.

The water between here and Texada Island is as calm as it gets. It would be a wonderful day to be on the chuck. I watch a small metal runabout with an outboard motor and a downrigger troll past the end of the old pier. A tug towing two rust-red flat (and seemingly empty) barges chugs southward, about a kilometre offshore.

After absorbing my welcome-home dose of Powell River, I drive back up the hill to the marine shop. This store has moved twice in the last two years and is now located two blocks above the pier. Previously, it was right on the wharf, sitting on blocks. Before that, it occupied a more permanent spot between the two harbours, commercial and transient boats to the south and recreational craft to the north. Another move back to the wharf is scheduled when the landfill project is complete. I've heard optimists say it will make Powell River's waterfront shops rival Granville Island in Vancouver. Dream on.

The lights are on in the store, but a *Closed* sign hangs in the window. An *Open* sign doesn't mean much in this town, so a *Closed* sign can be considered accordingly. It's worth a try.

The door is unlocked, so I step inside as the clangor rings its ding-dong tune. I hope Jim gets a bigger building when he moves to his next (and hopefully final) location. Every conceivable piece of marine gear protrudes from the narrow aisles. If you're looking for boat number decals, open the old walk-in meat locker and step inside. Jim's previous store was no bigger – to try on a pair of waterproof pants, you had to find the fishing tackle wall and swing it open, because that was the entrance to the fitting room.

Jim stands by the prawn traps, greeting me with a friendly "Hello" in his deepest Canadian drawl.

"Hi, Jim. I wasn't sure you would be open on a Sunday."

"Well, I'm not really open. I just came in to get some prawn bait."

I can tell he's glad to see me, but probably not enthused about being delayed from his prawn fishing.

"Oh, I'll come back tomorrow," I offer.

"No, it's not a problem. What can I help you with?"

"Just a tide book and some teak varnish, if you can recommend something for the wood trim on my Bayliner."

"Let me show you some stuff that I've found works good for sealing wood," he says, leading me back through the rope and hardware aisle. "When did you get back from the States?"

"Just arrived. Looks like you've got some good weather going."

"Not bad. Welcome back to our little backwoods community." Powell River has grown a lot in recent years, but people like Jim keep the town's characteristics personal.

Jim stops at a row of cans and runs his finger along the shelf. "Now where's that wood sealer? I think you'll find it's easier to work with than varnish."

The door clangor rings again, and Jim looks up from the shelves.

"Are you open?" asks a woman accompanied by a man and a pre-teen boy.

"Not really, but I'd be glad to help you," says Jim, as he hands me a plastic container of wood sealer and steps out of the aisle to assist the new customers.

"So what are you looking for today?" he asks the woman.

This would never happen in Los Angeles. You're either closed or you're open, nothing in between. Maybe this is one of the qualities that distinguishes this "backwoods community," as Jim describes it.

But if he ever plans to catch any prawns, he really should lock the door.

* * * * *

What is the order of the seasons? Does it begin with spring, or is it a never-ending cycle? Can the transition be noticed during a single day?

As September draws to a close, I plan a visit a nearby destination in the Strait of Georgia, a place I have wanted to explore for years. Why have I not already visited Mitlenatch? The island lies only 30 kilometres northwest of Powell River, an easy hour-long trip up the strait. But day trips have been increasingly uncommon for me in recent years, replaced by mini-voyages within the Strait of Georgia. Loading the boat for a day's trip is nearly as big a chore as packing for a week's journey. But today that problem is solved by tacking on an extra morning to a three-day trip to Prideaux Haven and Cortes Island. On the way home to Powell River, Mitlenatch requires only a slight deviation in course, and the elusive island is finally in sight!

Although it is in sight, herein lies the mystery of Mitlenatch – as you focus on it, the island appears to move farther away. Surely this is an old wives' tale caught in translation of the island's Kwakiutl name: "It looks close, but seems to move away as you approach it." I have purposefully focused on Mitlenatch for the past few kilometres during my approach from the east, and it doesn't seem to be getting any closer.

The island lies flat against the western horizon, catching morning sunlight that beams from behind the Bayliner. Vancouver Island forms the background for Mitlenatch, and that backdrop seems to be growing in size no faster than the mysterious little island. In the right season (not this one), they say you can hear the island before you see its prominent features, when the noisy seabird colony and sea lion haul-out add to Mitlenatch's mystique.

The elusive island sits within the changeover point of the mixing tides swirling around Vancouver Island. At the north end of the Strait of Georgia, water flows southward from Port Hardy. At the south end of the strait, the flow is northward after rounding the bend from Puget Sound. Mitlenatch sits where these tides meet, resulting in nutrient-rich water and a mild climate that gives the island its nickname, "Galapagos of the Strait of Georgia." Nestled in the rain shadow of Vancouver Island, Mitlenatch receives an annual rainfall half that of nearby Campbell River. The semi-arid soil even hosts prickly pear cactus. Unique factors combine to make this island a place that should not have been missed in my travels. Finally, I am here, or almost so.

Drawing closer (at least per my GPS track), the island's low-lying profile adds to the deceptive perception of distance. Mitlenatch's isolation from other landmarks also contributes to the illusion. The island certainly doesn't look like much from this distance – a flattened mound floating on the ocean.

The sea is nearly calm on this mid-September morning, so the island's northwest anchorage seems appropriate. We'll only be here a few hours, and a day hook should be adequate in these light swells. I wouldn't trust the northern shore in conditions less ideal than these, even though my boating guide indicates a shallow bottom with moderate holding conditions. Another First Nation's name for this island translates as "calm back end," but it is difficult to believe that the low-lying island protects the northern end very much during stormy southeast winds. Today, the northern bay is directly exposed to fair-weather northwest winds.

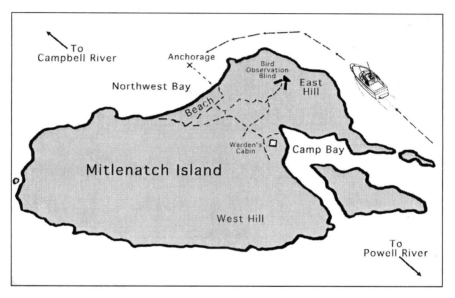

It's a beautiful September morning, an extension of summer that allows sunshine to penetrate my skin with near-burning warmth. Yet, as the Bayliner swings on its anchor, the air on the aft deck suddenly becomes cool as the boat's cabin blocks the sun.

Margy and I sit on the deck, relaxing and reading before going ashore. The fair-weather breeze is light, and the Bayliner holds nicely on its short rope. We are the only boat in the bay, and there is no need to rush this lazy morning.

Near noon, I prepare our dinghy, *Mr. Bathtub*, for the short trip to shore. There is no need for the motor today, so the preparation is simple. I load the oars and a light backpack containing my camera and a small bottle of water. Margy and I board the dinghy and head towards shore.

As I row towards the beach, the northwest winds aid my efforts, but I contemplate what would happen if these winds pick up. The trip back to the Bayliner could turn into more of a voyage than a jaunt. But the sky is blue, and the air is warm, banishing all thoughts of such problems from my mind.

The wide gravelly beach is at low tide, so I pull *Mr. Bathtub* well up the shore and tie his bow line to a log beyond the high tide mark. Grass and bushes begin immediately at the end of the gravel, stretching around the crescent-shaped beach.

The hiking paths are nicely marked, park-like and well worn by island visitors. There are no others here now, but it is easy to imagine the intrusion of people on this landscape during the earlier months of summer. What is also missing is the seasonal plethora of seabirds and wildflowers. I mentally mark the island for a return visit in the spring.

Margy and I climb the trail to the top of the bluff on East Hill and tuck into a wooden bird observation blind. Below us, a few gulls peck at the rocks, but this is undoubtedly far less than the usual level of activity that dominates this spot during the spring and early summer.

Leaving the blind, we pause to look down on picturesque Camp Bay and the warden's cabin. Beyond the cabin lie West Hill and the larger portion of the island, off-limits to visitors.

We descend the well-groomed path towards Camp Bay. Margy peels off towards the log cabin, while I return to the beach where *Mr. Bathtub* sits.

Waiting for Margy to return to the cove, I climb the low cliffs at the east end of the beach. I lay on a granite ledge, basking in the sun and watching the tide move up the beach. Just offshore, the Bayliner bobs in the gentle wind, and the day marches imperceptibly ahead. I try to envision the seasons moving forward.

My imagination brings me back to this spot in six months – in spring. But first will come autumn and winter, when the island sits deserted except for sea lions and a few birds. Through the winter months, Mitlenatch will continue its floating illusion in the Strait of Georgia, weathering the seasonal storms and awaiting the excitement of spring. I plan to be here to celebrate its return.

◊ ◊ ◊ ◊ ◊ ◊ ◊

Chapter 2

Savary Spring Fling

L ate spring and early autumn are my favorite seasons on the chuck. It has little to do with weather, although the skies and temperatures can be particularly enticing during June and September. Instead, it has to do with crowds; there are none.

Off-season boating in Canada doesn't have to be very off-season to make a huge difference. Even a few days before Canada Day helps. After that magic date of July 1 arrives, the local infrastructure of communities involved with boating on the Strait of Georgia changes dramatically. Before Canada Day, anchorages are relatively empty, and marinas and seaside stores are a pleasure to visit. In Lund, you can actually leave your boat tied to the fuel dock while you slip up to Nancy's Bakery for a snack, without even asking permission from the fuel attendant. Try getting away with that in the middle of summer.

As May transitions into June, there is an atmosphere of anticipation. Businesses may be on winter hours or even closed, but hammers are flying in preparation for the onslaught of the summer cruisers. In the Strait of Georgia, the anticipated boaters include Americans who traditionally head north in early July and return south in late August. The coastal boating network needs these visiting boaters, and profits significantly from their seasonal migration. But you don't have to love them. Said, of course, by an American who tries to pass himself off as a local.

In recent years, my boating on the chuck has been limited to off-season cruising as much as possible. My schedule as an author and publisher allows this, so I am quick to take advantage. In late May, I can sit at anchor in a nearly empty Roscoe Bay, with a few nearby boats barely making a dent in my feeling of privacy. The same anchorage in July is a maze of moored boats, with dinghies zooming back and forth, dodging closely spaced stern lines.

Besides the lack of crowds, May's cooler temperatures are a welcome relief. It's hard to find a truly hot day on the chuck except in July or August. I'll gladly ring the bell and wait for the fuel attendant in June or September. It's even fun to take a few minutes to lament the limited hours of the off-season cafe, its owners appearing to do everything they can to avoid prosperity.

* * * * *

From the balcony of my condo in Powell River this morning, I watch the ebbing water of a super-low tide. The rock breakwater towers over the harbour like a miniature fjord. It seems there is barely enough room to maneuver along the marina's inner wall. Yet, at this moment, the Coast Guard's *Cape Caution* blasts into the harbour without hesitation, its morning training exercise complete. The ship's broad wake stretches all the way back to Harwood Island.

It is the last day of May, and temperatures are expected to soar above 20 degrees C. The marine forecast calls for light and variable winds, with a shift to southeast tonight in advance of the next storm. If the weather holds, it will allow a day trip on the chuck, but the approaching storm will prevent an overnighter. It's a beautiful off-season day, but even for a brief visit to nearby Savary Island, it is prudent to keep an eye on the sky and an ear to the marine radio.

In the condo's downstairs storage shed, our bicycles hang by a mix of ropes and bungee cords, wedged above two 100 cc motorcycles. The bikes come down easier than they went up. I pedal down the hallway and precariously out the front door (watch those handlebars) as Margy walks her bike behind me. Then I coast downhill towards the marina, past the ferry terminal entrance. Going downhill, squeaky brakes proclaim a winter of inactivity for my bike. The final grade that leads to the marina requires me to lay hard on the hand brakes. I announce my arrival with a *screech-screech*, as I trade the noise for a semblance of control.

At the bottom of the hill, I decelerate the best I can in the wide paved area near the launch ramp. Jim, the wharfinger, is standing near the marina gate, watching (and hearing) my arrival.

"Hey, Jim, can I use your ramp for a water launch of my bike?" I yell as I swing past him.

"Have at it," says Jim. He probably wonders whether I am serious.

Considering the screech of my brakes, there may be no choice. But I point the bike uphill towards the elevated parking area beyond the ramp and receive a gravity assist in deceleration.

Now stopped and safely straddling my bike, I hop off and walk back to the gate.

"I'm headed to Savary for some biking," I explain to Jim.

"Good day for it," he replies.

"I know Savary's dock is reserved for the water taxis from Lund, but I figure I can use it to offload bikes."

"Sure. You can drop your bikes and tie up to one of the buoys near the dock. They don't mind this time of year."

Our conversation turns to Westview's planned marina renovations for the North Harbour. It's a major overhaul, designed to increase the docking space through a more efficient dock finger design.

"It'll be musical chairs for a while," explains Jim. "We won't be able to do it all at once. But we can bring the new docks in during the off-season later this year." He motions towards the north end of the docks: "Move all those boats to the other side, do the work, and then move them back."

It's an ambitious plan. This harbour is packed with boats. Installing more docks while keeping the marina operational will be an amazing feat. In recent years, the population of large recreational boats has increased. But this harbour is designed primarily for smaller craft. There are some open parking spots, but few of these spaces can hold the larger boats.

"The local boaters will be able to help," says Jim. "In the winter, some will be willing to take their boats out of the water for maintenance and temporary storage. It's the big boats that will be the problem."

True. What do you do with a 40-foot sailboat?

Margy joins us, having wisely walked her bike down the hill. We discuss the harbour plan a little more and talk about our cabins up the lake. Jim uses his float cabin mostly in the summer, and that time is fast approaching.

After our chat with Jim, a second trip back to the condo is required to load the supplies needed for the trip. Then, in the stillness of the super-low tide, we motor out of the North Harbour. We slip slowly along the breakwater's towering rock wall. You'll never see the tide lower here. I visualize the new moon, barely trailing the rising sun, pulling the ocean waters to a thin edge in this spring tide.

Exiting the breakwater, I keep the throttle at idle for a while. Sitting up on the command bridge, I take a few minutes to review a map of Savary Island. I don't feel comfortable tying up to a mooring buoy that may belong to a boater who is soon to return, so I inspect the chart for the best anchorage near Savary's wharf. The area surrounding the dock is advertised as "holding good in sand, depth 4 to 8 metres." Combined with the currently calm seas, these should be ideal conditions to regain my confidence in anchoring. So far there has been only one anchoring exercise this month, and it went well. But last summer's follies included a series of unsuccessful anchor attempts. Maybe it's just a down cycle on my nautical learning curve.

When I finally power up near Willingdon Beach, we pass behind a recreational runabout with a downrigger hoisted high. I give the small boat plenty of room for its salmon lure trolling peacefully behind.

Our boat is a 24-foot Bayliner Monterey, production date unknown (estimated 1987). The dingy is a small fiberglass catamaran mounted on the rear swim grid. The Bayliner a good vessel for us, although others might find it too small for cruises on the Strait of Georgia. Our friend, John, purchased this boat, *Halcyon Days*, for us as a transitional craft, meant to serve us until we can afford a bigger boat. Now we love it to death. How could we ever sell it and move up to something bigger?

A huge barge lumbers near the sand spit at Harwood Island. It seems too close to the sandbar, but it's undoubtedly only my perspective. From here, the gigantic floating flatbed looks like a conglomeration of old structures, reminiscent of giant pirate ships in the movie *Waterworld*. As we draw closer, it is only a large barge being pushed north by a tug, carrying closely packed cars and trucks.

Ahead of us, crescent-shaped Savary Island spreads across the horizon. I try to take a photo, but the island is already too big to fit in the camera's lens. So I wait until I round Mace Point and can view the island from a different angle. From this position, the island spreads westward, wrapping in its distinctive curve and fitting comfortably into the camera's viewfinder.

Beyond the point, the wharf pokes out from shore. At this low tide, the dock's large wooden pillars stand high above the water.

"I don't see how it's deep enough to dock," I remark to Margy.

"Around the other side, according to the map," she replies.

"The water taxis must use this dock at low tide," I suggest. "But they know the area a lot better than we do."

"We don't need to dock, if you want to just anchor and bring the bikes to shore by dinghy," she says.

We've already discussed this, although it seems easier to drop the bikes off first. *Mr. Bathtub* has never carried two people and two bikes. With the bikes, finding room to row will be impossible, so the extra weight of the Yamaha outboard motor will be also be required.

"It would be simpler just to anchor and go for it," I say. "If the weight seems too much, I could take the bikes to shore alone, and then return for you."

So our minds are made up, even before we check the backside of the wharf. I angle to a spot just outside the line of mooring buoys and drop anchor. It is one of those flawless maneuvers that makes you wonder how you ever experienced anchoring problems previously. But we have battled with anchors regularly, so we are pleased today is an exception.

I load *Mr. Bathtub* with our two bikes, the small Yamaha outboard, and the gear we need for riding. The motor starts on the third pull, a nice surprise after a winter of inactivity. Of course, it quits within seconds, but on the next start, it runs smoothly. I step aboard, with the dinghy still latched to the swim grid, nice and stable.

I'm not sure how low *Mr. Bathtub* will ride once I release the swim grid latches, so I do so carefully. Margy watches skeptically from the aft deck. As is often the case, she encourages me to slow my pace and to exercise caution, but once she knows I have properly considered the risks, she easily accepts the course of action.

As soon as the dinghy breaks loose from the Bayliner, it nearly swamps from the stern, weighed down by the Yamaha engine and me. I scoot forward, and *Mr. Bathtub* floats with increased stability. I carefully motor away from the Bayliner, executing a few simple turns to test the handling of the dinghy. Then I return to the Bayliner to pickup Margy.

"Step in carefully, and don't move around once you're aboard."

I don't need to explain further. Margy is concerned about this journey, but she's now willing to give it a try.

"If she flips, we'll be okay in this calm water with our life vests," I offer in encouragement. "Besides, it would be good for at least one chapter."

It's the truth. Some of my boating follies in Canada, initially discouraging, have made some of the best chapters in my books. It's a minor conciliation for incidents that I'm not very proud to acknowledge.

The trip to shore is slow. We plow water, but it is marginally safe. Margy sits motionless in the bow, which helps a lot, since I notice how even a minor shift in my weight causes an awkward tipping of the boat. Near the wharf, I experiment by pushing the throttle to its three-horsepower limit. The dinghy doesn't accelerate much, but it accepts the increase without swamping.

The shore is sandy-smooth, and we easily pull *Mr. Bathtub* up onto the gently sloping beach. With the dinghy out of the water by at least ten metres, I figure we can leave it, if properly lashed to the pier and secured from danger. Depending on how long we are gone, the rising tide may put *Mr. Bathtub* afloat, but I can always wade out to get him.

Margy secures the bow line to one of the wharf's hefty vertical pillars. She ties the knot as high as she can reach, over two metres above where she stands on the beach. Even if the water rises significantly, the dinghy will still float safely on its tether. When the tide is out, it is hard to imagine what the shore will look like at high tide. I try to picture it as best I can, consider *Mr. Bathtub* secure, and head for the road.

It is an easy walk through the brush at the shoreline. We step out onto the dirt road, pump up the tires of our bikes (which have been neglected for months), and start up the hill from the wharf.

"Why are islands always so hilly?" I ask Margy. "Maybe that's why they are islands" I answer rhetorically.

"It can't be as bad as Cortes Island."

Margy's statement refers to our grueling bike rides over the constant ups-and-downs of the roads near Cortes Bay and Gorge Harbour. Those bike rides were a constant battle with hills, although we keep returning to Cortes for the inspiring scenery.

Today, the first hill we encounter after leaving the wharf is impossible for either of us to climb on our bikes. I ride for a few minutes by standing and pumping on the pedals, but then give in to walking the bike to the top. Margy doesn't even try tackling the incline on her bike and begins a slow walking climb.

I arrive at the crest, near an intersection in the road, panting and sweating in the 20-degree air. An unusually high wooden bench perched at the side of the road seems perfect for an early rest. I park my bike on its kickstand, and climb onto the seat. Even a tall guy like me must look funny on this high bench, legs dangling in the air. A wooden sign next to the bench reads *Butt Stop.*

"Nice ride, so far," I kid, as Margy arrives at the bench.

"I hope it isn't going to be one of those hilly rides," says Margy.

"Thank goodness for a butt stop," I say, pointing to the sign.

Margy parks her bike and tries to heft her short body onto the tall bench. It takes two tries. We both look like munchkins on this high wooden structure, our feet hanging in midair.

After the initial climb and this well-deserved brief stop, the rest of today's ride is remarkably flat. Smooth climbs last only a short distance, followed by downward runs to gain momentum to tackle the next ascent. There are a few slopes where we need to walk our bikes, but the going is generally easy. On most of the island's stretches, we pedal without much effort. You couldn't hope for better on any island.

Our first navigational decision is where to go after the butt stop. There is a paved road to the right that looks flat and easy to ride. Straight ahead is an uphill grade, with a half dozen cars parked on the side of the road. Most of the vehicles are old clunkers, probably left by residents who are now off-island.

"I bet the main road is up the hill," I say. "I don't think we are high enough yet to be on the road that runs along the spine of the island."

Margy listens to my reasoning (which she later regrets) and follows me up the hill. It's too steep to ride, so we push our bikes another 100 metres to where the road bends right and levels. The next 200 metres parallels the street below, and then veers back down to join the lower road we started on. In other words, we made the climb for nothing.

At the lower intersection, I look back towards the butt stop. A truck has pulled off the road at a hanging sign advertising a pub-like cafe between the butt stop and us. I'm looking forward to a snack at the

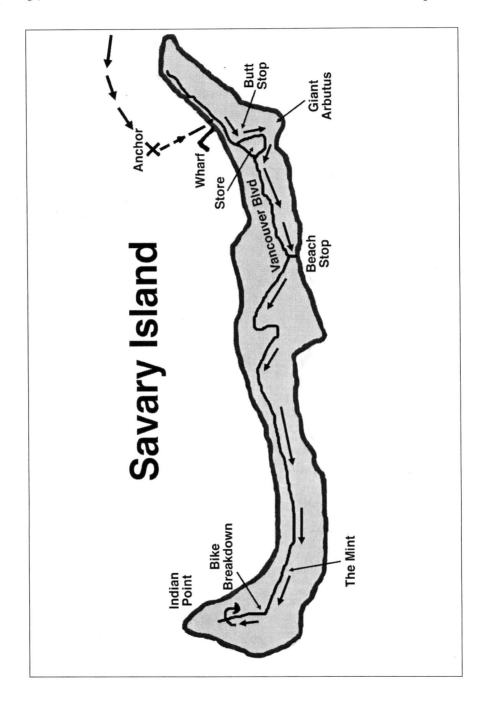

general store, and that should be only a little farther along this road. But I carry no map, so I rely on my memory of the island's layout from the chart left back on the anchored boat.

From here, we pedal along Vancouver Boulevard (a bit of a misnomer for such a tiny path) past small quaint residences and lots of new construction. The entire island seems alive with piles of lumber, a sign of the times. I get the distinct feeling that Savary is going through a growth spurt and that things will never be the same again. It's still a wonderful place, but as an outsider looking in, the changes seem obvious and somewhat ominous.

We pedal around the curve near the propane storage facility and start upward on an S-curve that should place us near the general store where I look forward to a snack. In fact, we have already biked farther than I expected for our snack stop. I'm sure we have already missed the turnoff for the "giant arbutus," a tree advertised as the biggest of its species. However, I have seen a lot of large arbutus, and I expect this one might be a bit of a disappointment by comparison. Often unadvertised creations of nature are more exciting than those listed on maps.

We take a break where a short trail leads to the beach. Here we are surrounded by bright yellow Scotch Broom with its pea-like flowers that spread upward from three-metre-high branches. This brightly flowering shrub is everywhere on the island, particularly along the edges of the road. It also dominates the plethora of May flowers in Powell River. I've never noticed such a lush crop of Scotch Broom before. This year, it has persisted in Powell River since my arrival the first week in May. Everyone says that spring flowers have come early this year, probably because of the heavier-than-usual rains of winter and the unusually warm air this month.

Scotch Broom is an amazing example of the rapid invasion of non-native plants. In the 1850s, three plants of this species were introduced on Vancouver Island. From these original imports, these bright yellow shrubs now thrive from Campbell River all the way down to Oregon. Scotch Broom has also crept up the BC coastline from Vancouver to Powell River, and it is now the dominant wildflower in the region.

Our ride from here is easy, but where is the general store? We wind through the island's preserved stretch of native forest, with its lush vegetation and moderately-sized trees, exiting this designated non-building area into a stretch of intense construction. The ruckus of sawing and hammering is everywhere. Blue tarps are set back from the road in many areas, covering large stashes of wood, soon to become houses. This island will never be the same again, and it's happening before our eyes.

I'm convinced that we're halfway across the island now, so maybe we should turn back. Of course, since the map sits back in the boat, I'm not sure where we are. As usual, I can't persuade myself to turn around until the terrain defeats me.

"When it starts uphill again so steep we have to walk, let's turn around," I say to Margy. She is quick to nod: "Yes." This is our first bike ride of the season, and it's a lot harder for her than me. I take advantage of the downhill slopes, letting gravity pull me along as fast as it can, in anticipation of the next uphill grade. But Margy is not as comfortable on a bicycle, feeling unstable and off-balance, so she brakes on the descents and has to work harder on the next upslope. Additionally, her shorter legs don't provide as much pedal advantage as mine, so she exerts a lot more energy on a ride like this. Margy is far from an "easy rider." On the other hand, she has relentless persistence. When the going gets rough, Margy gets going.

Another steep uphill grade doesn't occur, so we just keep on pedaling. It is obvious we have somehow missed the general store. We must now be well past the halfway point on the island, and that was not my intention. The island is ten kilometres long, and we haven't started back yet. This has become a major journey for us in our less-than-perfect riding condition. Still, we keep on pedaling.

Our ride is now downhill, past another settlement of houses and more blue tarps and fresh wood. Going steadily downhill is a nice relief, but we will have to climb this same road during our return to the wharf, so I resolve it is the end of the trail for us. Ahead, in the center of the road, a man walks with a large, long-haired black dog that leads him without a leash. I punch my rear brake once to announce my arrival – *screech!* The man looks over his shoulder and quickly hops to the side of the road to allow me to pass.

"I'm not as dangerous as I look!" I yell as I zoom past.

He laughs and nods at me. I raise my leg in anticipation of being chased by the dog, but I'm ignored. Now I lay on the brakes (*screech-screech*) and come to a stop at a bend in the road. Here the main road angles to the right and a smaller road leads to the left. At the intersection are a dozen wooden arrows on a single post. One arrow aims at Indian Point to the right. The old hotel, no longer in business, is located there, and it marks the end of the island.

The man and his dog approach the intersection, and I explain my downhill speed: "Sorry to pass you so fast," I apologize. "My brakes are making a lot of noise, so I didn't want to scare you."

"Not a problem," he answers. "Nice day for a ride."

"Yes, but I do have one question: Where am I?"

"You're at the end of the island," he laughs. "Indian Point is just around that curve." He points to the trail to the right.

"I didn't think I'd pedaled that far. I was looking for the general store as a landmark and never found it."

"It's way back by the wharf," he answers. "But it's closed off-season anyway. Are you staying for the night?"

We watch Margy gliding down the hill towards us. She seems to be coasting at an unusually slow speed and is not pedaling at all.

"No, we're headed back to our boat," I reply as we watch Margy. "If we don't run out of energy."

While we talk, I glance at my watch and compute the amount of remaining sunlight – still at least three hours. My thoughts are diverted to *Mr. Bathtub*. I try to redirect my attention to my conversation with the man, but my mind is on the dinghy. I've tried to ignore the thought until now, but it is getting late, and the tide must already be high. I visualize *Mr. Bathtub* tugging on his bow line, which might now be underwater. How much tugging before he swamps? At best, I expect I'll have to wade out (maybe swim) to retrieve the dinghy. And the wharf is at the other end of the island. This short ride has turned into a major challenge.

Margy joins us, carefully sliding off her bike. She points to her left pedal.

"Something is falling off," she announces. "And it's making a lot of noise."

I kneel down beside her bike and notice that the nut on the main sprocket is loose, dangling on the pedal bar. I fiddle with it, trying to get it back on the threads.

"Will you be okay?" asks the man.

"Sure, we're fine." I answer.

I'm confident we can keep Margy's bike operational for the trip back to the boat. And I'm relatively certain we'll make it back before sunset. But I hope *Mr. Bathtub* is still floating.

The man and his dog saunter off to the left, and I attend to Margy's bike. After wrestling with the nut for a few minutes, I finally realize it is reverse-threaded. Now it slides on easily. Since I have no tools, I tighten it as much as I can with my fingers.

"That should do for now," I announce. "We're at the end of the island, almost to Indian Point. We need to start back, but I want to try the road to Indian Point first. Why don't you wait here until I call for you? It's a bit uphill, and I'm not sure it's worth the effort." Margy quickly agrees.

In only a few hundred metres, the road starts moderately uphill. It's not a major hill, but I'm finished with unnecessary climbing today. I turn around and start back, meeting Margy at the intersection, where she sits straddling her bike.

"I didn't get to Indian Point," I tell her. "You go ahead. Start back to the boat, and I'll catch up."

I pull out my notepad to take some notes for this chapter. Since I ride faster than Margy, it will be easy to catch up.

After a few minutes, I am on the road again. I find Margy's bike parked at "The Mint," a bed-and-breakfast and oyster bar (in-season). She is talking to the proprietor and buying pop. She hands me a cold can of 7-Up, a well-earned and appreciated cool refreshment before we start back across the island. We drink our pop under a sign proclaiming *Rooms $10 per Night.*

"Hardly sounds like Savary," I note, motioning towards the sign. Maybe they put an extra zero on the price during the summer.

It's a long ride back. Although the road seldom requires us to stop and walk up hills, the pedaling effort is starting to wear on both of us. For Margy, her sprocket getting noisier, as if the chain is trying to shift gears but can't.

"Try moving the gear shift lever just a little while pedaling," I suggest. She does, and the sound gets worse.

At the turnout near the shore, we rest. I check her sprocket again, and it's evident that something is drastically wrong inside the housing. The main pedal bar wobbles loosely back and forth. It's amazing the bike can be pedaled at all, but Margy continues without obvious problems, other than the grating noise of the sprocket.

At one stop I say: "Try this," reaching down and flipping her chain off its sprocket to the next higher rung. You shouldn't be able to do this manually, an indicator of the severity of the malfunction. The change in the gear position does nothing to improve the situation.

I can't see inside the sprocket housing, so there is no way to tell what is wrong. One thing for sure – we'll need a bicycle mechanic when we get back to Powell River. Obviously, the first stop in town will be John's house. From bicycles to automotive repair to float cabin engineering, our trusty friend is an amazing coastal BC master of all trades.

In the last few kilometres leading to the dock, I take advantage of the downhill slope and my long legs. Meanwhile, Margy fights the clunking sprocket, the drag of brakes going downhill, and her shorter legs. But somehow she keeps making good progress.

Approaching the butt stop, I travel the short road segment we missed on our initial climb during our detour on the road above. In that 100-metre chunk of missed roadway sits the pub and the general store. Without a chart, we missed finding the elusive island store in the first few minutes of our bike trip.

I need my brakes to navigate the final hill to the wharf. *Squeak-squeal-squeak*. During the descent, I try to catch a glimpse of *Mr. Bathtub* between the trees. It is an anxious few minutes, but then the wharf is clearly in view. *Mr. Bathtub* floats tethered to the pier, bobbing on his bow line. The dinghy floats a long way from shore, in what appears to be very deep water.

The tide is still rising, but *Mr. Bathtub* is still floating. This might not last much longer. I can see the bow line, still attached to the pillar, but the rope is now stretched well down below the water. Time is wasting. Rather than wait for Margy, I decide to get started with the rescue.

I look around, checking for people on the shore. I'd don't see anyone. There is only one house in direct line-of-sight, and they are probably not watching me. A few boats float on moor lines nearby, but there is likely nobody aboard. I don't have another pair of pants or a spare shirt, and wet clothes on a cool spring evening would not be pleasant, so the best solution seems to be to take them off. I step behind a pillar that is not quite wide enough to block my body, and quickly strip.

I'm in the water, wading fast towards the cover-your-butt level. The sand is soft on my feet, and soon I am up to my waist. The water is cold but not excruciating. This island marks the mixing point of water flooding from both the south and the north around Vancouver Island, which accounts for its near-tropical conditions. I've visited the tropics, and this water certainly isn't tropical, but it also isn't bone-chilling.

I'm up to my chest and still a long way from *Mr. Bathtub*. The dinghy looks fine from this distance, bobbing gently on its bow line. I hop on my toes, thinking I may be able to make it to the dinghy without swimming. But soon the water is too deep, so I come off my toes and start to swim. In only a few strokes, I reach the dinghy, grasp the pillar, and begin untying the underwater knot.

Margy ties good knots, so you don't have to worry about them coming loose. I struggle with the knot, which is about a metre below the surface, reaching as far as I can without ducking my head underwater. Finally the rope comes free. I swim around behind *Mr. Bathtub*, and push from the stern in a dog-paddle towards shore.

Overhead, I hear the rumble of a vehicle on the wharf. A water-taxi must be arriving. Now another vehicle rolls across the wood planking, and then a third. What started out as an isolated, quick skinny-dip is becoming a bit more complicated.

The dinghy shields me from the house on the beach until I am nearly ashore. When the water gets shallow, I drop down and crawl on my knees, to avoid standing while pushing *Mr. Bathtub* farther shore-ward. Margy awaits me, holding my clothes, acting nonchalantly like this is the way everybody brings their dinghy to the beach.

This has actually been a great way to greet summer. The off-season lack of tourists doesn't bother me a bit. And it makes a bare-butt rescue of *Mr. Bathtub* a lot less stressful.

◊ ◊ ◊ ◊ ◊ ◊

Chapter 3

The Gemini Project

When you write a novel, so experts say, it should take shape as you go along. They also say good writers have a knack for letting their characters develop as the novel proceeds. You can't put words into a protagonist's mouth. If you do, it'll be the wrong words. Authors are as surprised as the reader regarding where the plot takes them.

I've written two full-length science fiction novels. Neither one of them has been published, which says a lot about their literary quality. However, I can verify that part of the fun of writing fiction is to let the plot go in whatever direction it decides. You can coax it, but you can't force it; otherwise, the fun of writing disappears. The same is true about many other aspects of life. Take the Gemini Project, for instance. It is a plan that starts big and grows even bigger, and the project follows the winding path of a developing novel. This concept involves a writer's cabin of a special type, and it certainly doesn't start with the title *Gemini Project* – write the title last, so they say.

The first criteria for my writer's retreat: it must be on Powell Lake. More specifically, it has to be in Hole in the Wall, easily accessible from Cabin Number 3. Of course, it has to be comfortable, in an environment that will inspire me to write.

Why isn't Cabin Number 3 itself sufficient for the task? In fact, my floating cabin is fully adequate, but it is also a bit crowded. This small structure isn't just my vacation cottage – it's my primary home in Canada. Margy and I get along well together in this confined space, but I desire a writer's cabin (or at least an area) to serve as a retreat, the kind of place you go to remove yourself from the hustle and bustle of float cabin life. Well, it isn't exactly hustle and bustle, but you know what I mean.

There are lots of possibilities, and I consider them all. The obvious is to build a separate mini-cabin on an attached float, sort of a floating in-laws' suite. John could construct this structure in style, and building it from scratch would allow a custom fit. But John isn't hot on the idea.

"There are rules, you know, about how many structures you can have on a single water lease," says John.

Since when is he concerned about rules established by authorities?

"And it would be expensive," he continues. "Just the float alone would be a big cost. It would be better to find something already built."

John is always looking out for expenses, and he is right that the cost would be high.

"But you could build a great writer's retreat," I insist. "The quality of your work has been proven to me time and again."

"Oh, I could construct it, all right. But what you need is something already built and ready to go, like a boat that's set up for ocean cruising."

It's a point well taken. John could refurbish a boat to meet my goals, all laid out just the way I want it. He's a master at any construction task, including the building of my floating cabin, beginning with the float itself. I'm convinced he's the world's finest aquatic engineer.

"Kind of like a floating RV," I say. "I could buy an old boat with a run-out engine at a good price."

What I really mean is John could buy such a vessel for me. I've learned my boat-buying decisions are best left to the most knowledgeable in my quasi-family.

"Take the Bayliner, for example," says John. "Imagine it docked behind the cabin. It would be nearly all ready to go."

"Or a houseboat," I reply. "They come with everything built in." I know little about houseboats, but the concept of such a vessel seems in-tune with my needs.

"If you can find one at a decent price. The *Penguin* is for sale, but it isn't much to look at."

When John's dad, Ed, was shopping for a houseboat years ago, he almost bought the *Penguin*. He changed his mind when he took it for a test drive. As a houseboat, it doesn't have the greatest stability. Ed explains how he thought the *Penguin* was going to overturn as he maneuvered back to the dock in a moderate wind. But the boat I buy will be sitting rather than sailing, docked behind Cabin Number 3.

I visit the *Penguin* at its Shinglemill dock. It's not in the "beautiful" category, but it has possibilities. For one thing, both ends are glass patio doors that provide lots of light and can be opened for flow-through ventilation. The interior would need to be completely gutted and redesigned, but I've watched John in action, and this he could handle.

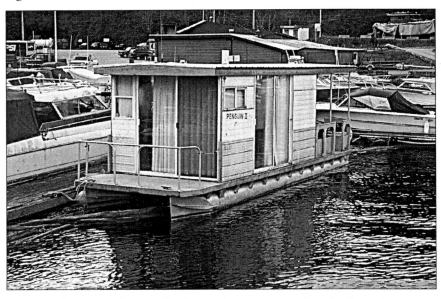

I make an offer on the boat (more correctly, the boat buyer in the family makes the offer for me), but it is a low bid, well below the asking price. The boat has sat at the Shinglemill with a *For Sale* sign for months, so I expect the offer to eventually be accepted. The owner never calls back. I consider this an indication that the boat may not be right for me. Sometimes things are just not meant to be.

Other possibilities arise, including a rumor that Jess might consider selling his float cabin, which is across the bay from mine. It's not much of cabin ("Eight by ten, just like a picture," chimes Jess), but it could be converted into a writer's retreat. However, it has solid walls, and how to convert it into an open-air retreat concerns even me (and I'm the guy who thinks John can do anything). Also, the location is removed from Cabin Number 3, although only a half kilometre away. I make an offer (through my Canadian agent, John, of course). In the spirit of coastal BC bartering, it's again low-ball, and Jess declines. I'm not really sure he wants to sell his cabin anyway.

Then Rick enters the picture.

Whenever you want to know anything about anybody or anything, ask Rick. Think about it. Who better knows a town inside out than a cab driver? He drives the streets every day, sees how it all fits together, and deals with a wide variety of people.

John tells Rick about my ideas for a writer's retreat, and Rick immediately finds a boat. The owner has to sell, since the boat is currently on blocks in the back yard of his rental house, and he's moving in less than two weeks. It's an old fixer-upper that was never fixed up.

"It's not much to look at," says Rick. "But it has classic lines, and the owner needs to get rid of it. You should be able to make a good deal."

What Rick really means is he can make a good deal. The situation must be treated gingerly, says Rick, but he could buy the boat from the owner for me.

I drive to the owner's address with John, park intentionally well past the driveway, and sneak into the backyard. No one appears to be home. The boat is not really a secret, since you can see it from the driveway, but there is no *For Sale* sign. We want to look at the boat without dealing with the owner. After all, Rick is the potential buyer.

I fall in love instantly. Even from a distance, the boat overwhelms me — an old classic design, almost tug-like — and it's big.

Boats on blocks always look bigger. A boat out of water looks massive by virtue of the increased surface area you see that would normally be hidden below the waterline. This boat looks huge (in reality, it's only 22 feet, shorter than my Bayliner), and it's a classic flat-top. Such a design is not what I'd want in a cruiser, since I'm a command bridge enthusiast these days. But this boat has a different purpose. I visualize the top as a sundeck, with a solar shower hose running off the roof. I picture myself taking a warm shower on the aft deck between writing sessions.

The rear deck is wide open, and that is good. But it is wider open than desired, considering the condition of the stern. In fact, the aft deck doesn't exist. You can look right down to the hull. The rear of the boat and the cabin interior are trashed, with metal, wood, and fiberglass flung everywhere. But this boat has possibilities.

What it doesn't have is an engine. The cylinders for the diesel stern-drive are lying in the bilge near the transom, making an oily mess. But who needs an engine? All I need is a watertight hull. When the stern-drive leg comes out, there will be a big hole to fill, but it can be plugged.

The name stenciled on the boat is *Gemini*. John likes that, since he is a Gemini. I like the fact that John likes it.

Rick makes an offer, and it's accepted. Where else could you find a diesel cruiser for $500? The price tag is a good indicator of how much work will be needed.

The owner needs it hauled away by the first of the month. We have nowhere to put it.

* * * * *

We entertain many ideas about where to put the boat, but none of them work out. Finally, we buy some time. On the last day of the month, while I am in California, John arranges to have the boat moved to a local marine storage area. The boat sits on blocks, awaiting its assigned priority by for engine removal and sealing of the stern.

The plan is to make this boat watertight, and then tow it to John's Cabin Number 1 for refurbishment. Maybe we can arrange to do some of the initial refurbishment at the Shinglemill Marina first. Traveling seven kilometres up the lake every time you need to work on the project will not be convenient.

As the boat sits on blocks awaiting the sealing of its hull, a new possibility emerges. The Flying Club is renting hangar space for RV and boat storage in an attempt to meet expenses, although a boat on blocks is not currently on the club's list of rental considerations. I could probably arrange to expand my current hangar space to a hangar-and-a-half. This would be a secure location for *Gemini*, with protection from the weather, and there's electricity for power tools.

When the boat shop is finished sealing the hull, John arranges to move *Gemini* to the airport. Even with a recent expansion of my hangar rental space, there isn't enough room for the Piper Arrow, a trailer with two quads, a promotional bookmobile (*Mr. Float Cabin*), the Campion's trailer, and a boat on blocks. So the airplane gets evicted. An anti-moisture light and desiccant crystals, aided by the fuselage tarp, keep the airplane relatively dry in its new home, outside on the tarmac. The Arrow sits at the corner of the Flying Club ramp, next to the club's Cessna 172, where she has good neighbors and a nice view of the activity at the clubhouse. The Arrow reluctantly puts up with the indecency of being evicted from her hangar by non-flying objects. (The following year, a premature and costly engine overhaul will be partly attributed to the torture of winter when parked outside on the wet and cold BC coast.)

The first major step is to tear out *Gemini's* interior. In the first days of grunt work, Margy and I make a lot of progress. She tackles the demolished aft deck, which is currently little more than a trash bin, and I start work inside the cabin. We decide to strip the interior right down to the floor, although we haven't yet determined how the solid cabinet structure will be removed. The cabinet supports are fiberglass-molded directly into the hull, but John says he can take care of this with a power saw. It's hard to visualize how it will all be accomplished, but we just start ripping things apart, not worrying about the details.

While I tear away the sink, stove, and wiring, Margy removes the remaining engine parts from below the deck near the stern. Then she works in the rear of the cabin, pulling out the toilet and its associated plumbing. Despite her small stature, she does more than her fair share of the manual labor. She's the kind of team worker who spurs you on to work harder yourself.

It's a lot more work than I anticipated. So much work, in fact, that one night at John's house we entertain some alternatives. It is not yet too late to divert this project towards a different course. We're headed for a complete renovation of the boat's interior, stripping everything to the hull, turning a classic old boat into a flat-floored writer's retreat. The targeted product is not unlike a houseboat in function, so maybe it would be easier to turn to a boat better suited to that design. Another boat, nearly ready-to-use, might be cheaper in the long run, or maybe a houseboat should be reconsidered as a solution.

There are a lot of boats to consider, including a multitude of won-derful-sounding deals listed in the boat trading journals. John always has an eye out for old boats, so he already has some candidates. The problem is that most of the deals sound too good to be true; they probably are.

John recommends a local boat for consideration. It sits next to the fuel dock at the Shinglemill and has displayed a *For Sale* sign for months, along with another poster proclaiming *For Charter*. I've noticed this boat before, and it seem a prospective candidate. Its rear deck is big, as is the command bridge, and the aft cabin wall is mostly glass. But it has twin engines (we need none), so I expect the cost to be outrageous; but it isn't.

"It's priced to sell," says John. "He just wants to get rid of it."

The only major question is whether it's configured properly. A charter boat might already be stripped inside to carry more passengers, and this boat is big, at least as wide as *Gemini* and four feet longer.

John and I meet at the Shinglemill to inspect the boat. I arrive first, and have already seen everything I need to know. The interior is in reasonable shape, but it is not stripped as expected. Instead, it boasts a sink, stove, and head, just like *Gemini*.

When John pulls up in his truck, Bro bounds out of the driver's door. It is a flurry of flying dog (big dog) clear across John's lap and out onto the ground. Bro sprints directly towards me, demonstrating his ability to immediately hone in on his target.

Bro runs around me in circles, leaping and barking, as I try to calm him down. This only increases his jumping dance. John saunters onto the dock to join us.

"What'ya think?" he asks.

"Good boat," I say. "But it's pretty much stock inside. Looks tough to tear apart."

John walks along the dock, inspecting the boat's hull and interior.

"Lots of space inside," says John. I know he likes the concept of twin engines, although we have no plans for using either of them. "But it just isn't for you, is it?" he adds.

John knows me pretty well. He can probably tell by my tone, or maybe by my posture.

"No, it isn't what I want."

"There'll be others," he says.

I'm amazed how easily he lets go of this boat. My prepared arguments aren't necessary. After a few minutes we leave the dock, discussing what other paths this project might take.

"Maybe I had to see this boat to convince myself we are headed in the right direction," I reason. "I do love *Gemini's* classic lines."

"Don't forget about a houseboat," John reminds me. We are supposed to be rationally reevaluating the whole project before committing to refurbishing *Gemini*.

"I haven't forgotten," I respond. But in my mind, it seems that the decision to proceed with the Gemini Project is easier now.

"Let's look at Joe's houseboat, even though it's not for sale," John says.

Looking at boats of any kind is an activity John and I can pursue all day long. There's just something about docks and boats.

Joe's houseboat is near the end of the last dock finger. It takes us a while to get there, so we talk as we walk.

"It seems insane to buy another boat," I say. "What will we do with *Gemini*? We've sealed off the hull and pulled out most of the wiring and plumbing, even the throttle cables, so putting an engine in would be a major job. What could *Gemini* be used for?"

"We could haul our quads on it," John says, with anticipation in his voice. "Don't need an engine – we can just tow it."

"True, but isn't that the idea behind the old boat parked at Cabin Number 1?" I ask. That project has been in-the-works for several years, with only one quad trip on it so far.

"*Gemini* is an even better design for hauling quads," replies John. "I could build ramps to load from the dock – just ride our bikes aboard!" His mind is in overdrive now, and that's hard to stop.

Joe's houseboat is more like a house than a boat. As we walk alongside it, I visualize a houseboat parked at my cabin – a big boxy trailer that doesn't seem as exciting as *Gemini*. A houseboat is a design that has its place on a lake, but it isn't at all like *Gemini*.

"You can keep looking at boats for me," I conclude. "But I think I'm okay with *Gemini* now."

John understands. He nods his head, acknowledging that the path is set. I hope there will be no more turning back.

* * * * *

The next day is a late-January terror. The wind howls, and the rain blows fiercely in nearly horizontal sheets. It's a good day to work on *Gemini*. The hangar, although open in structure, is well protected from the rain.

Using a stepladder, Margy and I climb aboard, crawl over the aft rail, and then take the long step down to the floorless hull. We stand deep within the aft portion of the boat, with only fiberglass lying between us and the future water below. From down here, I can barely see over the transom.

I hook up the worklight and begin preparing the cabin for the next step – John's attack with a power saw. I unbolt the captain's chair and rip away the sides of cabinets, trying to remove as many of the big structures that I can.

Meanwhile, Margy does some final cleanup in the back of the boat, tearing out a rotted wall panel from the rear of the cabin. I want more glass, so that will be a good spot for a new wall with a window.

As we work, the wind whips up from the southeast, pushing through the open-ended hangar. Every once in a while, a gust grabs *Gemini* and tugs her with a jolt. I think about the precariously placed wooden blocks on which the boat sits. Our added body weight today provides more stability than *Gemini* has experienced in recent weeks. Still, I wonder if we will go airborne and then crash to the hangar floor.

Above the roar of the wind, I hear a turboprop approaching. I walk forward to the boat's windshield to watch a Pacific Coastal Beech 1900C smack unceremoniously onto Runway Zero-Nine, directly in front of the hangar. It isn't a pretty landing, but it's under control, and that's the important part. The aircraft's thrust reversers are barely needed to bring the twin-engine airliner to a stop in the strong wind. I try to imagine landing here today in my Piper Arrow, and quickly dismiss the thought. Landing in a strong crosswind, with the windsock straight out and gusting from side-to-side, is not my idea of enjoyable flying. No one would try a takeoff or landing in a small airplane at this airport today.

I watch the Beech 1900 as it taxis to the terminal, quickly exchanges its passengers, and taxis back for takeoff in front of us.

"You've gotta see this!" I yell to Margy. She comes forward from her teardown project at the back of the boat, and we watch in awe as the twin turboprop gets airborne in only a few hundred feet of runway. As soon as the aircraft breaks ground, its wings rock furiously back-and-forth in the gusty conditions, until the airplane disappears into the low overcast.

"Imagine flying that airplane today," I remark. "Any airplane, in fact."

"Not me," replies Margy. "I'd drive to Vancouver first." That's six hours, including two ferries.

What happens next is beyond belief. While Margy returns to the rear of the boat, I hear a small engine to the side of the hangar. I stretch my neck forward against the boat's windshield and catch sight of a yellow single-engine Cessna taxiing in the grass. After rolling only a few metres, the nose of the airplane drops sharply downward, the prop almost hitting the ground. The pilot guns the engine, but the airplane won't move. He shuts down, jumps outside into the nearly horizontal rain, and inspects the nose landing gear. Apparently finding no damage, he hastens to the tail of the aircraft, laying his full weight on the horizontal stabilizer. This is an acceptable technique, when used carefully, to turn a small airplane around in a tight spot. But it never works for me. My Arrow is heavier than this small Cessna.

The pilot is persistent. He leans on the tail, and rotates the Cessna 45 degrees in the muddy grass. Then he gets back aboard and restarts the engine. Surely he is merely repositioning his aircraft, maybe bringing it into a hangar and out of the storm. There is no way he is going flying today.

But I am wrong. He guns the engine and manages to get out of the muddy hole he has dug with his landing gear. Then he enters the taxiway and heads towards the runway. This guy is going flying!

"Get up here right away!" I yell back to Margy. "This guy thinks he's going flying in a Cessna 172."

What could possibly be important enough for a takeoff in a small aircraft under these conditions? This is clearly a recreational aircraft, with no markings to indicate a commercial charter. To be pushed to safety limits by the mighty loonie is one thing. To go flying for personal reasons on a day like today is insane.

The airplane proceeds to the end of Runway Zero-Nine, just out of sight beyond the hangar wall. In the gusting wind, I hear the Cessna completing its engine run-up, and then the yellow airplane darts down the runway. It doesn't dart for long, since the wind is so strong the plane is airborne in only 200 feet of runway. The high wings seem to flop back and forth on the struts, as the small airplane flounders upward more-or-less to the east. The Cessna enters the clouds (and the structural ice within!) and is gone.

In all my days of airplane watching, I've never seen a takeoff like this. Wherever he's going, it sure must be important.

* * * * *

Even after we are far into the Gemini Project, I still waffle in my decision. John tells me the *Mugwump* is for sale (again) at the Shinglemill. I considered buying this boat several years ago, when it was previously for sale, as a potential vessel for use on the ocean. It's interior roominess and classic design make it half houseboat, half cruiser. Fortunately, John steered me away from buying this boat for the ocean: "You'll kill yourself on the chuck with a boat like that," John declared.

But could I now use this boat for a different purpose? It's available right here in Powell Lake, and that convenience rears its head as additional rationalization for buying it.

John favors the design of the *Mugwump* as a writer's retreat, but I am not convinced. There is a special beauty to the boat and her funky design, but she doesn't fit the function of a writer's retreat. I walk along the Shinglemill dock and gaze into the boat's interior, trying to visualize the *Mugwump* moored alongside my cabin. I nix the idea, and John doesn't question my decision. That undoubtedly means he isn't convinced either. So we commit to *Gemini* once again, and this time there will be no turning back.

* * * * *

While I am in California, John begins his major assault on *Gemini*. He strips out what remains of cabinets and cabin structure. He repairs rotted spots in the floor and begins the final repairs to the hull. The boat is sealed for launch, but there is a lot of fine-tuning yet to be done. John sets a Tuesday-Thursday work schedule and slowly plods along with a project that is bigger than either of us imagined.

The Gemini Project proceeds like a novel with a plot that is developing ever so slowly; like a protagonist without form. But we will carry *Gemini* through to completion. It had better be before this book is finished.

Chapter 4

Thud Ducks and Glow Fish

Today's tides are influenced by the new moon. An especially low tide will make the entry to Roscoe Bay a particular hazard. If we are to enter, it cannot be at low tide. The next high tide is near sunset, so that becomes the targeted arrival time. To complicate the schedule further – the next morning's exit must also be at high tide.

This will be my fourth visit to Roscoe Bay, depending on how you count. Each was memorable in its own regard.

On the first visit, John took me on a grand tour of Desolation Sound that he carefully rehearsed (in typical John-style detail) by making a trip the previous day with his friend, Doug. As spontaneous as John may appear, he prefers setting a plan in cement before acting on it. Since he is not an expert regarding Desolation Sound, he chose Doug to assist him.

The next day, in the 17-foot Houston, we cruised through Thulin Passage, separating the Copeland Islands from the mainland, on the start of an all-day tour of Desolation Sound. Roscoe Bay was first on the list.

That summer day, we entered the bay during a fairly low tide, with a rocky underwater shoal acting like a tidal gate. John tilted the outboard motor upward to assure proper clearance of the bottom. Meanwhile, dinghies zipped back and forth, challenging the shallow entrance as they whizzed past us.

Roscoe Bay's entrance opened up into a panorama of boats anchored everywhere. Stern lines predominated, allowing maximum capacity in the sheltered cove. Near the center of the bay, boats were rafted up to each other, while dinghies darted to and fro. Music of mixed genres wafted from boat speakers. It was the epitome of popular summer anchorages in British Columbia – a beautiful summer day to visit the human zoo.

My second visit to Roscoe Bay was during an off-season solo trip in early June, with pleasant overnight weather. Only a few boats were present, so I anchored the Bayliner in a wide, secure spot just inside the bay. I swung on anchor without interfering with anyone or risking contact with the shore.

During the night, I awoke to the sound of thuds against the hull. Not loud thuds, but thuds nevertheless − as if the boat was being whacked by small logs.

I extracted myself from the V-berth, slowly sliding rearward on my back, thus avoiding my tendency to hit my head on the instrument panel overhead beam. I stepped out onto the aft deck with my flashlight, and watched the ebbing tide flow past the Bayliner. It was an obstructed flow, carrying chunks of "something" that (at least in my imagination) was alive. With my bright-beam flashlight, I inspected the nearby water. What appeared to be floating by was...

A multitude of ducks. It seemed impossible, but the objects thumping against the hull every few minutes sure looked like small ducks − dead ducks, floating on their backs with their legs high. Or was it my imagination?

Dead ducks being pushed against the hull − *thud, thud*. I remember an anxious sense of fear, wondering if what I saw was real. Could something be killing the ducks and washing them out of the head of the bay or down the stream from Black Lake above the bay's inlet?

I didn't want to look at dead ducks any more, so I turned off my light. I simply went back inside the cabin and tried to go to sleep. In a few minutes, the sound of ducks (or wood) whacking against the hull ceased. The thud ducks were gone, but not forgotten.

On another solo trip to Roscoe Bay, I waited somewhat patiently at the entrance one evening while high tide approached. I had arrived early, with lots of time to kill; for a while, the wait went smoothly, as I fished at nearby Marylebone Point. The setting sun blazed through the opening in the mountains behind Roscoe Bay and its narrow eastern entrance, spilling onto the Bayliner.

While waiting, I fished in deep water, jigging off the bottom. On my second cast, I caught a fish, and it was a big one. Unfortunately, it was a rockfish, raised from 300 feet. I should have known better, since rockfish (red snapper) are often caught at this depth, and they seldom survive the decompression forces during the ride up to the surface.

I wanted to release the fish, but its air bladder was too bloated to allow the rockfish to swim. I tried cutting a small slit in his protruding bladder with the sharp point of my knife. I've heard this allows rockfish to return to the depths again, as evidenced by fish occasionally caught with healed slits in their bladder. But it is probably not an adequate solution. On this disturbing evening, I spent an unhappy half-hour trying to resuscitate the fish by pushing him back down into the ocean with my fish net. The rockfish would briefly swim away, half righting himself, only to flop upside down, nearly lifeless. Eventually, the fish disappeared, maybe under the boat and then lost in the waves. Possibly (I'd like to believe) he made it back to his family below. In any case, I was devastated by the incident and didn't want to hover at this entrance any longer.

So I bolted for Prideaux Haven, easily reaching it before sunset. An evening at majestic Prideaux can revive even the most depressed spirits, and it did so for me that night.

I never visit Roscoe Bay without a memorable incident. Yet, to me, even with the thud ducks and rockfish, it is still a beautiful place. I don't hesitate to go there again.

* * * * *

This evening, the high tide will arrive shortly after 9:30 pm, as predicted by a quick look at the Powell River tide tables. It will occur a few minutes later at Roscoe Bay, which I plan to verify by consulting the Canadian government-issue tide charts before entering the bay. The spring tide (new moon) will be one of the highest of the month. With the shallow draft of the Bayliner, I can safely enter within an hour either side of high tide. In fact, that is being cautiously conservative.

Sunset comes late now, only three weeks before the longest day of the year. Sitting at the entrance to Roscoe Bay this warm evening, awaiting entry, will be enjoyable, but I won't arrive so early as to risk catching a deep-water rockfish.

Being early turns out to be a non-problem. Instead, we are running late. Margy and I have been on Savary Island most of afternoon, and we'll need food for tonight. The first stop is Lund, a good place to buy dinner supplies at the general store or a meal to-go at Nancy's Bakery.

As we approach the fuel dock, a large sign proclaims *Winter Hours 8 – 4*. It must still be winter, although I wear my shorts and T-shirt in the warm air of early evening. It's a good thing we don't need fuel, since winter hours in Lund apparently extend to the beginning of summer.

We secure the Bayliner next to a metal-hulled crew boat, the only other visitor at the dock. Then we climb the ramp up to the hotel. Lund looks like a ghost town in the setting sun. The front of the hotel is boarded up, a victim of an attempt to renovate the harbour-view rooms in time for the tourist season. They'd better hurry.

"How about Nancy's?" I ask.

We'll find dinner snacks at Nancy's Bakery. I love the pizza. Who needs a grocery store?

"Sure, if it's open," replies Margy.

Guests lounge on the deck of the hotel, so Lund isn't a complete ghost town, but there is little other activity. The ice cream store is closed, and Nancy's looks dark. Margy and I walk closer to see for sure. On our way to the bakery, we pass the boat launch ramp, where fishermen are offloading prawns from a boat into a pickup truck. Margy lingers behind, watching the prawn fishermen, while I walk ahead to the bakery.

"Closed," I yell back to Margy, once I get close enough to read the sign in the door. "Must be winter hours."

The general store is still open, but one attendant is vacuuming, and the other is tallying the coins in the till. We will be their last customers today.

At the deli counter, we grab two fresh looking sandwiches in plastic wrap, a small tub of potato salad, and a slice of apple-rhubarb pie that is marked down to 99 cents. On the way to the cash register, I grab a bag of chips.

"How's this for an elaborate dinner?" I ask, as the blond woman rings up the bill.

"It would work good for me." She smiles as she puts the items in a plastic bag.

"The best part is doing the dishes," I add.

We exit the store to the sound of the vacuum belting out its closing-the-store tune.

* * * * *

Leaving the harbour, I point the Bayliner's bow to the outside of the first island in the Copeland chain.

"Let's go outside and around," I say to Margy. "It'll be faster – we can cruise as fast as we want."

The inside route, through Thulin Passage, would mean slowing to minimum wake if there are boats at anchor. When in a hurry, the long route is sometimes faster. It's still not too late for high tide at Roscoe Bay, but the sun's angle is getting low. It would be nice to be in the bay before sunset to enjoy the twilight.

We cruise past Bliss Landing and around Sarah Point into Desolation Sound. The water is calm, and we are comfortably up on-plane. I point the bow outside Mink Island to avoid the rocky area on the far end that requires extra vigilance. My GPS receiver, back at the factory undergoing warranty work, is sorely missed. The portable unit is a great piece of equipment that is shared between aviation and nautical duties. But it has suddenly stopped working for the second time in less than a year. Without it, we'll be safest on the outside of Mink Island.

Our cruise from Lund to Roscoe Bay takes only 45 minutes at 20-plus knots. We round Marylebone Point at about eight o'clock, still over an hour before high tide, based on my rough computation using Powell River's local tide chart. There is no need to wait. The water sits just shy of the high-water mark on the rocks; the entry shoal will be well submerged.

I follow the recommendation of the cruising guide and navigate to the left of center during the initial approach. Then I slip into idle and angle towards the middle of the channel. From the command bridge, it is easy to survey the entrance for obstacles. As we pass over the narrow bar, all is clear for a good distance on both sides.

Inside the bay, early evening sunlight slashes through the mini-canyon. Shallow ripples on the water catch the light like wrinkled foil. A sailboat and a powerboat are visible at the far end. We continue ahead 100 metres inside the entrance, where the cove to the right opens to reveal another sailboat. But that's it: three boats and us in paradise. It's totally unlike the crowded days of summer.

I reverse course and drop anchor at the same spot as my previous thud duck visit. As the anchor goes down in 30 feet of water, I let out extra rode, and Margy backs the boat towards the center of the bay. She handles the boat expertly in close quarters like this, allowing the anchor to grab promptly; we are secure.

The wind is light from the west, but the drift is in the opposite direction on the rising tide. I pull out the official Canadian tide tables and compute high tide. Roscoe Bay is not a designated reporting station, but using the tide computation for nearby Prideaux Haven, I find a 13-minute additive factor to the Point Atkinson high tide time. The front of the book clearly tells me to add an hour for daylight savings time. That brings the predicted high tide computation to 10:44 pm, slightly over an hour later than listed in the unofficial Powell River tide booklet. Powell River's tides are also based on Point Atkinson, and the add-on factor there is five minutes. So why over an hour's difference between the two tide charts? I conclude that Power River's local booklet doesn't compensate for daylight savings time, but I find nothing to warn me of this. I'd like to verify my conclusion by observation. At 9:30 the flow is still inward, although very slow. Soon thereafter, I am sound asleep.

* * * * *

I awaken just before 2 am and climb out of the V-berth to check the night sky. Forever an avid amateur astronomer, I can't resist the stars.

Observing from the aft deck, high clouds allow only the brightest stars to shine through. Flashes of light in the water behind the boat catch my eye. I've seen reflected stars in the water in dark places before, but these are not reflected stars. Whatever they are, they are flashing and moving.

I allow my eyes to adjust. Streaks of light radiate out from both sides of the stern. Some flashes dart in zigzag paths in (or on) the water, quick blue shafts of light, noticeably fluorescent. This must be living organisms – hundreds of such creatures, all tiny and fast moving, emitting short bursts of light all around the boat's stern.

As one of the tiny blue lights winks on, I shine my flashlight down towards the water; the light is gone. Another blue streak, and I swing my light to the spot. This time, it looks like a small fish just below the surface. Or is it my imagination? Could it be bugs on the water, zooming to and fro like water striders? No, these creatures are moving too fast for water bugs. It is all so quick – a glowing streak a few feet long for a few seconds, more streaks; and then they are gone.

I consider waking up Margy to see this, but decide not to do so, since the light show now seems to be over. It will be tough to describe this dazzling event in the morning.

When I reenter the cabin, Margy hears me and knows I have been outside checking the stars.

"How's the sky tonight?" she asks groggily.

"The sky is boring, but the water is plenty interesting."

"Not thud ducks, I hope," she replies.

"Better than that. Come take a look."

Back on the aft deck, the action has begun again.

"Could they be jellyfish?" asks Margy.

"They move way too fast for jellyfish. Notice how they dart and change course so quickly."

"It might be the water itself, with algae that glow when fish swim through," guesses Margy. "Maybe it has something to do with the tide, since it looks like there's a bit of a current."

"That makes more sense than anything I've thought of."

We watch in awe for another half-hour, and then the darting luminescent streaks dissipate to almost nothing, so we go back to bed. At least it's not thud ducks.

* * * * *

The next morning, I prepare to take a water sample once we are outside Roscoe Bay. I'll use the Kemmerer bottle I've brought along on this trip. It's one of my first attempts to use this scientific metal pipe-like container that I've borrowed from a friend. I've also packed my microscope aboard to study the samples. I want to test the Kemmerer bottle in a 90-foot drop into salt water (I have only 100 feet of the proper rope) in preparation for a pending 1000-foot drop onto the floor of Powell Lake.

But as I organize my equipment, I realize a sample drop would be in vain. I've brought along the drop bottle, its accessories, and the microscope, but I have no microscope slides or cover slips. The test drop will have to wait for another day.

I turn my attention to the tide table dilemma. The disparity in times still bothers me, but I settle on a way to resolve it. The next predicted high tide (per the local Powell River table) is approaching in only a few minutes. The official Canadian tables (with an hour added for daylight savings time) indicate high tide is still over an hour away. So I'll just watch the flow and see what happens.

For now the tide is still flooding into the bay. Leaves on the water are flowing inward, although there is no wind. Jellyfish are riding the rising water, their Saturn-like disks pulsating as they drift by. These are the most active jellyfish I've ever seen. On this flood tide, they are ceaseless in their undulating invasion of the bay.

I take the time to absorb my environment, as I should do more often. I like to think I am good about paying attention to the details of my surroundings, but the truth is I am usually in too much of a hurry. Today I take the time to linger on the aft deck, watching the water. Margy and I have our life vests on, the cabin is secure, and we are ready to hoist anchor. But I do not move. Margy is used to my of-ten-hurried nature, and she obviously enjoys this change of my modus operandi. She waits patiently, without question.

The high tide, per the Powell River booklet, is well past. Still, the flow continues. By 7:41 am (the time of published slack tide in the Canadian tide tables), the inward flow has not yet ceased. I double-check my computation: 6:28 for Point Atkinson, plus 13 minutes for Prideaux Haven (the closest location on the tables), plus an added hour for daylight savings time. In fact, at 8:00, the inflow is still evident, although considerably slower now. Of course, this is not Prideaux Haven, but twenty minutes later than predicted seems excessive. Is the science of tide prediction so inexact?

Meanwhile, I scan outside the bay's entrance. I'm looking for a line on the water. Isn't a narrow entrance such as this a perfect setup for a tidal surge? The only time I have witnessed such a phenomenon was in Bute Inlet on the lucky day *Mr. Bathtub* encountered a salmon (*Up the Lake*, Chapter 14). I'd love to experience such an unusual flow again, so I periodically gaze out the entrance. There is no tidal surge, but a large sailboat is tacking back and forth in front of the bay – north and out of sight, then back south to disappear again. Well, it isn't exactly tacking, since its sail is stowed, but it is moving under power in a similar pattern. The boat appears to be waiting to enter the bay at exactly high tide. Its deep keel needs all the water over the rocky bar it can find.

This sailboat provides another hint regarding the mystery of the tide tables. The Powell River booklet is obviously in error by over an hour, partly due to lack of (documented) correction for daylight savings time. The official Canadian tables are also a few minutes late regarding this high tide, probably due to location error (Prideaux Haven is six kilometres away). Yet somehow this sailboat knows it is not yet high tide. Since he is under power, it is unlikely the skipper is able to visually determine the tidal flow. He must have a more accurate tide table than mine that provides the proper correction for Roscoe Bay. Maybe he has a GPS receiver that shows local tidal data. None of this makes a lot of sense, since tide tables are tide tables. There is only so much data, and it is all based on the official Canadian tide charts.

Nevertheless, at 8:10, a half hour after the predicted tidal peak (over an hour and a half after the Powell River computation), the flow of jellyfish slows almost to nothing. In fact, the current is arguably sideways at the moment. It is now that the sailboat changes course from its north-south passes to travel in a swift and sure line towards the entrance to Roscoe Bay. The large sailboat maneuvers slightly south of centerline into the deepest water and then heads straight towards the submerged entry shoal.

This is no ordinary sailboat; in size alone, it is very large.

"It has a cross-bar on its sail," notes Margy.

Yes, it is a large mast, with a large cross-bar, now empty of sail.

"Looks like a pirate ship," I reply, as we watch it maneuver into the bay.

I visualize the deep keel crossing the rocky shelf, clearing it by only a few feet, even at this high tide.

"Not only does it look like a pirate ship, it is one," says Margy.

What is she saying? Oh, now I see the black and white pirate flag flying behind the red and white Canadian colors.

As the sailboat passes, it's obvious this is not a pirate ship, although it is of that design. The financial value of this boat would be enough to keep any pirate satisfied for years, with no need for piracy.

We wave; they wave. The large sailboat slips into the solitude of Roscoe Bay at the peak of high tide.

These "pirates" know about tide tables. Maybe it is just one of those things only skippers of big ships are meant to know.

Slack tide has arrived. The only movement in the water is the spreading wake of the sailboat now pointed directly towards the head of the bay. I am finally ready to leave.

"Let's raise the anchor," I announce.

I slide along the side railing and onto the bow. Simultaneously, Margy takes her position on the command bridge. She turns on the blower, primes the engine with a few shots of throttle, and engages the starter. The engine starts immediately and idles steadily.

On the forward deck, I pull our boat over its anchor using arm-over-arm retrieval of the rode. Then I wrap the rope around the winch drum in a single loop and hit the foot switch. The anchor breaks loose from the bottom and comes up smoothly. I motion for Margy to start out of the bay. She angles directly for the entrance, while I pull the anchor aboard and stow it in its metal rack.

As we motor slowly towards the entrance, I remain standing on the forward deck. Usually, I immediately return along the catwalk to join Margy for the exit from an anchorage. Today I remain on the bow, caught up in this morning's absorb-it-all attitude. I stand and gaze at the water below. I watch the rocks to the sides of the boat, although it is not necessary for safety during a high tide exit in this shallow-draft boat. But I stand, watch, and absorb my surroundings. It provides a few moments of extended serenity within this always-memorable destination – Roscoe Bay.

Chapter 5

Field Reporter

In recent years, John has taken a boat trip on the chuck each autumn; a voyage in the Bayliner to explore coastal BC. He takes along a friend, provisions for several nights, and two 100 cc motorcycles. Autumn is a quieter time along the coast, and John is quick to take advantage of it. The recreational boats are gone, and the weather is still magnificent (as long as you keep a weather eye on the Aleutian low-pressure systems).

As plans for *Up the Strait* progress, I come up with an idea. With an empty spiral notebook for ammunition, I drop in on John one day at Cabin Number 1. It seems as good a day as any to plead my case.

"I have a present for you," I say as we relax on the deck in the late September sun. John rests on his, plastic chaise lounge, absorbing the afternoon rays. I lay comfortably flat on my back, next to him on the wooden deck.

"Your presents can mean trouble," replies John.

My presents can be suspicious. Some of my off-the-wall ideas begin with bribes.

"Well, I didn't just think this one up. I've been pondering an idea for my next book, and I need your help."

"What now?" asks John with a disinterested tone. His eyes are closed, but at least words are coming out.

"Here's your present."

I reach into my pocket and hand him a miniature, black spiral notebook. John reaches down towards the deck to receive it, and sets it on the arm of the chair without opening it.

"It's blank," I note.

"Great. Just what I needed."

"Well, I got to thinking about your trip on the chuck." John's eyes are closed, but I know he is missing nothing. "Take this notebook with you and write some stuff down. I'd like to develop it into a chapter for my next book."

"You're the writer, not me," replies John. "What would I write?"

His reply isn't an outright "No," so I'm encouraged.

"You don't have to write anything fancy. Just jot down a few notes, some words to get me started. I've been known to make up stuff as I go along."

"That's for sure," says John, with a distinct note of sarcasm.

"For example, maybe you'll just write down 'Big waterfall,' and then I can ask you more about it when you get back. As your trip proceeds, give me some thoughts, and I'll take it from there."

"Okay, I can do that," says John.

I'm surprised and thrilled. I didn't expect such outright coopera-tion.

"And don't forget to take some pictures. Scenery and equipment shots – you know the type. A few photos with people are okay – like the photo you took of Eldon on your trip to the head of Jervis Inlet."

"That giant cedar, with Eldon's arms spread out – quite a tree," says John.

"Yes, exactly. So you're okay with this?"

"Yup. I know what you need."

This is amazing. John actually seems enthusiastic, in his own sub-dued manner. But I anticipate a blank notebook when he returns, so I give him an incentive to fill up the pages.

"Here, take this too," I say, reaching into my pocket. I hand him a standard borrowed-from-somewhere pen. "I don't want you to have any excuses."

* * * * *

The weather doesn't cooperate. When I telephone John from Los Angeles, he laments about the endless rain. To compound the weather dilemma, his planned journey requires travel on a weekend, since he will be tying up to logging docks. Most logging docks are available to the public only on weekends. As autumn creeps in, the chances of a fair-weather weekend get ever slimmer.

Like any BC resident, John acknowledges that adverse weather must be accepted in this region: "You just gotta expect it," he says. But I muster hope that the weather will break for him soon. It doesn't.

* * * * *

When I return to Powell River the second week in October, southern BC is being inundated with wave after wave of rainy weather. I sneak in, flying my Piper Arrow through the Pacific Northwest between major storms. It's lucky I arrive when I do, because the skies begin to pour the following day, and it doesn't let up for almost two weeks.

One rainy afternoon, as I leave John's house, I notice the little black notebook perched on the dashboard of his truck. It stands ready for an adventure that has never developed. But blank pages can stand empty for a long time and still eventually be covered with tales full of adventure.

The notebook remains on the dashboard, but the trip is canceled by the stormy autumn weather. Fall turns into winter, and eventually into spring. The spring situation is no better. John's plan to take Doug along with him on the boat-motorcycle journey complicates matters. Doug's work schedule at the paper mill conflicts with the timing of the few weekends of reasonable weather. Summer arrives, and the situation improves. In late August, both weather and work schedules finally align appropriately.

* * * * *

Almost a year late, John and Doug finally load up the Bayliner.

John pulls into Marine Traders, where I'm promoting my books. We converse in the parking lot, near John's truck, while *Mr. Float Cabin* (my bookmobile with a Powell Lake decor) awaits the arrival of the next ferry. In the back of John's truck sits a huge plastic water container. Several bags of potato chips protrude from a brown paper sack.

"Do you know if there's a can opener in the Bayliner?" asks John. "I couldn't find one at home." Maybe his menu is even more elaborate than chips and water.

"I'm sure there is, probably in the silverware drawer, under the table."

"We're just about loaded," says John. "The bikes are aboard, and we should be able to leave this afternoon."

"That means you'll be tied up to the logging dock on a weekday," I observe.

"There's no logging at the head of Jervis this week," replies John. "So we'll be okay."

How does he know these things?

John and Doug plan to ride the trails north and west of Jervis. They've talked about trying to make it up to Ice Lake on the side of Mount Alfred. What they find there will be important information for the Powell River ATV Club, whose members have been working on a trail just west of Mount Alfred for months. If John and Doug can find a way around the mountain on the south side, it will be worth pushing the trail through from the west. Their ultimate goal is to blaze a quad trail all the way to Squamish. The government has been talking about building a road to Squamish for years, without any real progress.

"Do you have another notebook like the one you gave me last year?" asks John. "I left it on my dashboard, but now I can't find it."

"I don't have one handy, but you could just find a big piece of paper and use it instead," I suggest.

"Suppose so. But I'm not sure I can find a pen either." Surely he's kidding.

"Bring me back some notes, no matter what," I demand. "Even just a few words will do. Like 'I saw a bear today.' And I'll take it from there."

"Sure. I'll do it."

My field reporter climbs into his truck and rumbles off towards the marina. I hope he finds a pen.

* * * * *

Six days later, John returns with notes for the author. What began as a three-day trip gets extended, as John and Doug find multiple places to explore in Jervis Inlet. Besides checking out the head of the inlet and making an attempt to reach Ice Lake, they broaden their exploration to other bays along the way.

"Here's my log," John announces proudly, handing me the black notebook. "Doug helped, by reminding me to write in it every night. We took pictures too."

It's the original notebook I gave him a year ago. He found it after all. Apparently, he also located a pen.

* * * * *

That evening, I thumb through the notebook. The first few pages are notes to himself over the past year: dimensions of lumber, hardware lists, and some long-hand math. His to-do list includes: "Buy plywood for Elizabeth's planters."

Finally, the first page of his trip log begins: "Captain's Log – Stardate 3042.6. We have entered the twilight zone and are ready to lay cable."

This is going to be an interesting trip report.

* * * * *

"Boat so heavy with gas and supplies that it barely got up on-plane. Doug went into the bow to help during acceleration."

The two 100 cc motorcycles take up the aft deck. Together they weigh 330 pounds, the equivalent of two extra people sitting on the stern. When you're trying to get on-plane with full gas tanks, it's almost impossible.

The entire front deck is taken up by Doug's Zodiac, which restricts visibility when driving from inside the cabin. Like me, John prefers the command bridge anyway. With the Zodiac up front, anchoring is difficult, but all of their overnight stays will involve mooring to logging docks or booms.

The weather on Jervis Inlet is typically challenging: "Three-foot waves on the way up; calm past Patrick Point."

The next morning, things get off to a bang.

"Started breakfast. Doug walked up the road to go to the bathroom. Came running back. Grizzly with three cubs eating blackberries only 200 feet from boat."

Unlike the common black bear of the Powell River area, grizzlies can exhibit a mean streak. They tend to be tolerant of humans, but don't mess with them when their cubs are nearby.

Doug adds a few comments in his own penmanship: "Mother Grizz stopped when she saw me, and stood up on her hind legs. One cub was in the blackberries close to me. So mother came to protect it. Watched bears for a few minutes."

Typical reporters' conflict: Doug says he watched; John says he ran. Maybe a little of both.

When confronted, a grizzly typically stands on its hind legs to survey the situation. When I see the photo, I accuse John of taking a picture of Doug in a bear suit.

The original goal of finding a route to Mount Alfred and Ice Lake is thwarted by the terrain: "Rode bikes most of the day. Couldn't find way to Alfred. Will try again tomorrow."

At the head of Jervis Inlet, big trees spread everywhere. Old-growth cedars are the giants of the region, and John appreciates their awesome beauty. At one stop, Doug snaps a photo of John at the trunk of one of the bigger cedars.

While the Bayliner is tied up to the logging dock, "rich Americans" in a Seattle-based 60-foot tour boat anchor nearby. Their large dinghy, *Island Spirit*, is experiencing engine problems when it comes ashore.

"I volunteered Doug to tow them back to their mothership with our dinghy, while I ate supper." (Never interfere with John's supper.) "Doug came back with strawberry shortcake and two litres of milk." (Rich Americans.)

Later that night: "Thought I saw a bear; just mother raccoon and three babies."

John and Doug bike extensively along the trails at the head of the inlet, each time coming to a dead end in their attempt to reach Mount Alfred: "Went up to Lausman Main. Major cross-ditches. Hiked up to waterfall and found a narrow canyon with a massive rock wedged across. Drove up another valley, and went as far as we could. Overgrown. Arrived back at boat – grizzly with two cubs at dock."

Bears are a common sight near the logging dock: "On the way back from the Hunachein Valley, I decided to go back to the boat to check how rough the water was. Doug was up another road. I was stopped by a grizzly with a cub. The damn bear wouldn't let me pass. After a few minutes, I finally got by."

* * * * *

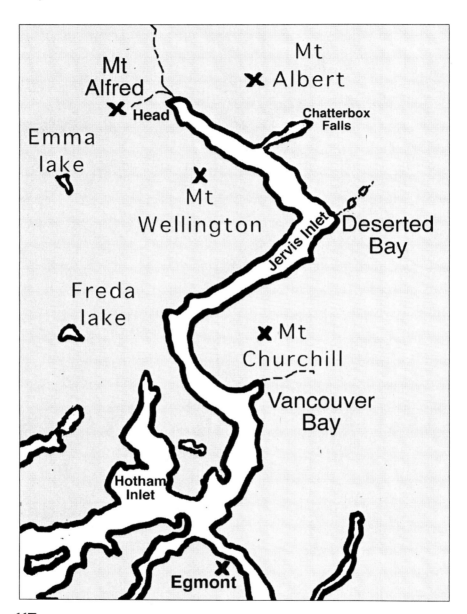

"Loaded up boat and drove to Deserted Bay. Rough ride, big time. Tied up to small dock, unloaded bikes, and went for ride. Good road except for a few cross-ditches. At one ditch, we had to pull bikes up with a rope."

On this ride inland from Deserted Bay, John and Doug find two lakes. The first lake has remnants of old logging activity. A train trestle still runs across it. The second lake is mysteriously dry. John and Doug hike around the lake, and fail to find either an inlet or outlet. The next day, they return to the first lake to get a photograph of the trestle. They meet two First Nations hikers.

"They told us that the second lake was affected by the level of the tides. This lake is ten kilometres from the ocean." One of the natives (Spooner) explains that a lava tube feeds water to the lake, even this far from the ocean and at an elevation of 1000 feet.

The First Nation hikers also provide some history of Deserted Bay: "Called 'Deserted' because all of the people died, except one," says Spooner. The lone First Nations survivor was found at the settlement and transported to Sechelt. Blankets provided by missionaries were blamed for the spread of smallpox among everyone in the village.

* * * * *

"**D**eparted for Vancouver Bay. Got halfway. Had to tie up to log boom near a glacial creek due to rough water. Finally made it to Vancouver Bay in time for supper." Don't mess with John's supper schedule.

The next morning: "Having breakfast, while a seal is eating a salmon next to the boat." Sounds like an appetizing sight during breakfast.

The log camp's caretaker, Tommy, stops by. He provides John and Doug with a tour of the camp. Tommy lets them use his telephone to call home, but they fail to make a connection.

Then they go riding again: "Saw some elk."

John's reporting style is exactly what I want. His matter-of-fact account of the details of the trip are John-like in every aspect. He is an individual who appreciates what he sees. He grasps the beauty of the sublime.

On the sixth day, John and Doug load the boat for the last time.

"Early start for home (7:50 am) to miss the rough water. Good ride back."

"Stardate 3048.3. Captain's log complete."

◊ ◊ ◊ ◊ ◊ ◊ ◊

Chapter 6

Sea Lion Day

As a February morning dawns, I stand behind the patio door of the condo, watching the Comox ferry slip past Rebecca Rock (*Becca*) and angle towards the ferry dock at Westview. The *Queen of Burnaby* plows nearly directly towards me, suspended on flat, dark gray water against a backdrop of sun breaking through clouds behind.

I slide back the patio door to test the temperature, and a barking chorus of California sea lions cuts through the cold morning air. It is now mid-season for the winter visit of these noisy animals. Those I hear this morning are at the paper mill's pond, three kilometres from here. These sea mammals are clearly of the California breed, distinguished by their barking. Steller sea lions, the other prominent species in this area, roar rather than bark. I wouldn't be able to hear their growl from this far away.

As an example of migratory resolve, only male California sea lions winter on the British Columbia coast. The females remain in rookeries a thousand miles to the south. In May, the males will leave coastal BC and migrate to California to find the females. In October, the bulls make the long return trek north, leaving the females to tend the rookeries.

I call today Sea Lion Day, a self-proclaimed date to visit the local sea lions at two of their favorite haul-out sites. The goal today is to observe both California sea lions at the mill pond and Stellers on Mitlenatch Island.

* * * * *

The seas are fairly smooth as Margy and I motor out of the marina. It's best to expect anything this time of year, but the marine forecast indicates acceptable conditions, at least through the afternoon. The swells are still from the southeast after yesterday's storm; gentle rolling now, with the wind expected to shift to the northwest as the day progresses. The previous day's fury of wind and rain has roared past us and into Washington.

Margy and I ride on the command bridge, bundled up in our heavy jackets. I wear a full-face ski mask, and Margy uses earmuffs to fend off the near-freezing temperature. Almost nothing, not even the cold, can keep us from the command bridge. It is much easier to see the waves and dangerous flotsam from up here, and maneuvering this boat from on-top is a joy. From our high vantage point, we approach the mill pond, outlined by the hulks of old concrete ships, decommissioned and now aligned to form a breakwater.

About 15 California sea lions are perched on breakwater rocks, concentrated near the entrance to the mill pond. They raise a rough barking chorus as we approach, their voices echoing off the nearby hulks and the cliffs at the shore. The sea lions hold steadfast on their haul-out spot, a line of rocks that extends towards the beach, forming the edge of the millpond.

Closer to the breakwater, I slow to idle and shift into neutral, reducing our noise footprint enough that only one sea lion decides to escape into water. He slides in, maybe for reasons unrelated to the approach of our boat, and bobs a few feet from the breakwater. I stop the Bayliner near the tip of the rock wall by briefly shifting into reverse, then back into neutral, letting the boat drift on the gentle waves. Our cameras are clicking, and the sea lions are staring and barking. Their blobby brown bodies seem to be posing for our cameras.

As we drift closer, I back slowly away from the rocks. Then it's back into neutral, gliding gently on the waves. A touch of power will position us perfectly for photos, so I slip the gearshift forward. A resounding *crack* erupts from the fiberglass dinghy stowed on the stern. And the engine immediately dies.

I try to restart the engine, perplexed by the cracking noise, but the shift lever is jammed in forward. The engine will not start in this position, and this usually indicates something is caught in the prop.

Margy is already down on the aft deck, taking pictures. I follow, climbing down the ladder from the command bridge two steps at a time.

"What was that noise?" I yell.

"Don't know – maybe we caught a rope in the prop."

"How can that be?" I lament. "We don't have any ropes in the water."

"We do now," replies Margy. "There's a blue rope stretching right down to the prop. It looks like it comes from *Mr. Bathtub*."

Now I see the blue rope, one of the ropes from the dinghy is now taut, leading directly towards the prop. That explains the loud *crack* – a rope from *Mr. Bathtub* wrapped itself around the prop and tried to pull the fiberglass dinghy down and away from the aft railing, where she is tied. Either the railing or the fiberglass is cracked, hopefully not seriously.

Meanwhile, we are drifting directly towards the rock pile. We'll come very close to the colony of sea lions, maybe hit the rocks, or (almost as bad) drift into the mill pond. This is private property. I picture armed guards watching us closely from the mill as we drift into their sacred territory. Maybe they have gunboats, ready to launch. I have an active imagination.

I'll need to reach into the water up to my armpit to get to the prop, and that's unlikely to resolve the situation anyway. I've had ropes around the prop before; it isn't a pretty picture once they get past the prop's seal. And with the dinghy in the way, there's no way to even get to the prop.

"Let's lower *Mr. Bathtub*!" I order.

Margy is already untying the dinghy. As soon as the knot comes loose, I push outward on the fiberglass shell, and *Mr. Bathtub* plops unceremoniously into the water. The splash causes most of the sea lions, now looming ever larger as we draw closer, to slip into the water without a lot of finesse. These huge animals splash around, right next to us, and I don't like the thought of these big creatures being so close. I doubt they are naturally mean, but we're messing with their haul-out area in a big way.

The largest sea lion of all remains steadfast on the rocks. He looks like he isn't going to desert his territory without a fight.

We're just off the point now, only five metres from the rocks, and I must reach down into the cold water, into the crack between the swim grid and *Mr. Bathtub*. There's no time to do any more in preparation than push my jacket sleeve up a few inches.

Meanwhile my mind races with thoughts of what to do if I can't pull the rope loose and restart the engine. There's always the dinghy's tiny outboard, a three-horsepower Yamaha that's perfectly suited for *Mr. Bathtub*. It's also supposed to serve as an emergency kicker in case the Bayliner's main engine dies. It could never handle rough seas. I've only mounted it once on the stern for a test drive. But it might get us back to the nearby marina in these nearly calm conditions.

Then, of course, there's John. My satellite phone stands ready to call for help. John would get here fast. In fact, even a cell phone should work from here. There's something comforting about the idea of John handling an emergency like this, so I concentrate on that thought, as the rocks loom even closer.

I reach into the water behind the swim grid as deep as I can. The water is cold, but my jacket and glove help protect me. I come within inches of the rope, but can't quite grab it.

"I need something to reach with!" I'm trying to stay calm, but I know I am snapping orders. "Maybe one of those stakes on the command bridge will be long enough."

I hear Margy fumbling around, but it sounds like she is in the cabin rather than on the command bridge. I continue to reach downward as far as I can. In the water, my arm is magnified, and my hand seems just inches short of the jammed rope.

"How's this?" asks Margy, as she hands me a broom.

I grab it and shove the handle into the water. It touches the rope, and I twist the broom handle to allow the rope to wrap around it. Got it!

I ease the rope towards the surface with the handle, careful not to let the line fall free. When I am able to grab the blue rope in my hand, I pull as hard as I can. Nothing happens. I give it another frantic tug, trying to get the prop to rotate. This time I feel the rope move the blades a fraction of an inch. Another firm tug, the prop rotates, and the rope comes free.

"Got it!" I yell. "Let's get outta here!"

But now, with success nearly in sight, I spy the biggest of the sea lions looming in front of me. I can almost reach out and touch him, as he stands proudly, ready to defend his rocky perch. There's really nothing this huge California sea lion can do in defense of the Bayliner's approaching momentum, but he isn't about to give in to the crisis. He rears his handsomely-rounded head into stiff profile. It's a warlike pose for an animal that probably weighs over 500 pounds.

This is a classic photo op that may never come again. I immediately clamber up the steps to the command bridge in search of my camera.

"Hey, where are you going?!" yells Margy. "Help me with *Mr. Bathtub*! We're going to hit the rocks!" Every clipped sentence is evidence I'm abandoning my post, but I must get this picture.

We are almost on the rocks, as I grab my camera and click the shutter. The sea lion simultaneously tosses his wet head in defiance, and water sprays onto me in a shower of drops that announces a proud moment in this animal's life. The sea lion stands his ground – an awesome sight. He is a warrior who owns this pond.

"Get back down here and help me!" demands Margy.

If we're going to hit the rocks, it is now too late to do anything about it. But we luck out and are pushed harmlessly past the breakwater entrance by the waves, clearing the end of the rocks by only a metre. We drift untouched into the mill pond.

The crisis now behind us, I assist Margy with raising *Mr. Bathtub* and then climb back up onto the command bridge. I shift into neutral, and the engine starts on the first try. As we exit the pond, I glance back over my shoulder at the smoke-spewing mill buildings. I wonder if a guard with a semi-automatic has us in his sights?

As we pass the entry rocks on our way out, the victorious sea lion is gone. With the battle won, he has slipped into the water for a well-deserved morning swim with his family of admirers.

* * * * *

We settle in for the ride to Mitlenatch Island. I expect to find Steller sea lions there, so it should be an interesting comparison of the two haul-out locations.

I navigate past Sliammon, giving wide clearance to the sand spit at the eastern tip of Harwood. Almost immediately after clearing the spit, Mitlenatch is visible in the distance. It is still a long way ahead, but it sits as a distinct dot on the horizon just to left of Savary. The speck seems in the right location, based on our GPS track. Within a few miles, the island begins to grow in size. I remind myself this small island traditionally provides a deceptive scale of distance, seeming to drift farther away as you approach it, but for now, it is growing larger rapidly.

The waves are growing fast too, but I'm sure there will be shelter on the backside of Savary Island, if needed. From there, it would be an easy detour to the safety of Lund Harbour. The sky ahead remains mostly sunny, with the surface winds continuing from the southeast in the wake of yesterday's storm. A few isolated whitecaps indicate the wave height is approaching three feet, but we are still within the comfortable limits of the Bayliner. I'm not sure Margy agrees, as she holds on tight while we pound across tightly-spaced trailing swells.

Occasionally, the waves drop to a more comfortable height, but simultaneously logs float in a line to our left. It is old, smooth wood, not the type to come loose from a tug's boom of logs. The severe winds of the previous day have pulled logs from the shorelines throughout the Strait of Georgia. Chunks of wood ranging from large logs to kindling have settled into lines of drifting debris. I angle to the right to avoid the wood, and that points us towards Savary on a track that will need to be altered to clear the tip of the island. When the line of flotsam doesn't end after another kilometre, I turn nearly 90 degrees to the left, reduce power to idle, and prepare to cross the nearly solid line of logs.

As we approach the line, I can see that it is less than 50 metres wide, so I throttle up briefly, and then cut power to idle. I attempt to drift through the wood as far as possible in neutral, with the prop stopped to prevent damage.

We don't make it all the way through, but another brief burst of power pushes us out the other side into clear water. This is only the first of many such lines of floating debris that will plague us all day. Our travel comes in segments of on-plane cruising, intermixed with short spurts of crawling through calm areas where the flotsam accumulates.

Mitlenatch is now right off the bow, maybe five kilometres away. Make that ten – as advertised, the island approaches and retreats, seeming to float between the surface of the water and the lower reaches of the sky. It has a mirage-like appearance at times, and the sun angle (from a low winter sun) adds to this enchanting effect. Others have described this experience with Mitlenatch as a shrinking and expansion of the island, even a splitting of the island, depending on the light and sea conditions. It is not an erroneously described effect. It may only be an optical illusion, but the deceptive perception is almost mystical in nature.

As we draw closer, Mitlenatch finally takes on the appearance of a standard rocky island. I now feel confident in judging my distance as two kilometres. We are approaching from the southeast, so I decide to circumnavigate the island anticlockwise (counterclockwise for my American friends), expecting to find the primary sea lion haul-out near the eastern tip, partly because of the rocky bluffs on that end of the island. Also, on my previous visit to the island, I gazed down from a bird blind on what looked like ideal sea lion territory at the eastern tip.

Within a kilometre of the shoreline, I come off-plane, reducing speed to five knots. We'll respect the 300-metre marine park limit, using binoculars to view the sea lions.

But the highly indented east edge of the island is uninhabited today. The rocks look perfect for sea lions, but no one is home.

As we round the point, still motoring slowly, the gravel beach of the northern bay comes into sight. On the far end of the beach, there is a sudden ruckus. Sea lions pour off the beach and into the water. I shift into idle and grab the binoculars. At least fifty sea lions pound through the water in a splashing mass along the shore. Even at this distance and our slow speed, our boat has spooked them. These are not at all like the mill pond's sea lions, who refused to budge until we were on top of them. Obviously, they are not used to people visiting their winter habitat.

The throng of splashing sea lions disappears around the promontory to the west. A few brave souls stay behind at the gravelly beach, but a couple of minutes later, even these slip into the water and join the exodus.

After letting things calm down a bit, I motor slowly along the shore. When we round the point, sea lions are everywhere. Their huge bodies bask on the rocks in the on-and-off beams of sunlight that break through high clouds. Some of the sea lions rest a few metres above the shore on rocky ledges. Others bob in the ocean a little farther up the shore. This time our boat causes little reaction. I slide slowly ahead to a good observation point between the sea lions basking on the rocks and those swimming contentedly farther up the shoreline.

When I shut off the engine, I can immediately hear them breathing – rough snorts, then heavy breaths. But they are not barking. They wheeze and grunt rather than bark.

These are even bigger animals than the California sea lions at the mill pond. Their bodies are substantially grayer, and I estimate the weight of the biggest as nearly 1000 pounds. Using the binoculars, it is clear that their heads are of a more angular shape. These are Steller sea lions (more correctly, Steller's sea lions, named after a biologist who studied the species) in their winter home.

Steller sea lions (also called northern sea lions) depict a sad lesson regarding human stupidity. In the 1920s, thousands of BC sea lions were machine-gunned to death under the leadership of federal fisheries employees. Stellers were hunted nearly to extinction under the banner of saving the salmon industry. The only good news is that a subsequent biological study showed that sea lions are opportunistic feeders, consuming some of the enemies of salmon (such as eels). This information came nearly too late, but soon enough for a harsh lesson regarding upsetting the delicate balance of nature. The remaining Steller population received a last-minute reprieve. However, during the period of slaughter, an environmental niche was opened for California sea lions. They moved into many of the territorial waters of the Stellers, where they have co-habited ever since.

We spend nearly an hour drifting and watching the Stellers. Most of them bask on the rock shelves. One occasionally climbs clumsily over his neighbors and slides into the ocean in a semi-agile slither that diminishes the splash of such an enormous body entering the water. The sea lions already in the water bob back and forth in a small area near the rocky point. It is an interesting example of muted colony socialism. Somehow, regardless of size and power, everyone seems to get along.

When we are ready to depart, I decide to continue our circuit of the island a bit farther to see if there are more sea lions, but we find no others here today. Although many of the rocky bluffs seem ideal for these animals, the entire colony has congregated in the small area now behind us.

Before completing the circumnavigation of Mitlenatch, I break off and point the bow of the Bayliner at the smokestacks on Vancouver Island. Campbell River is close, and this seems like a good time to visit. There is still plenty of daylight left, and the seas are cooperating. It is warmer now, the sun beaming down onto the command bridge.

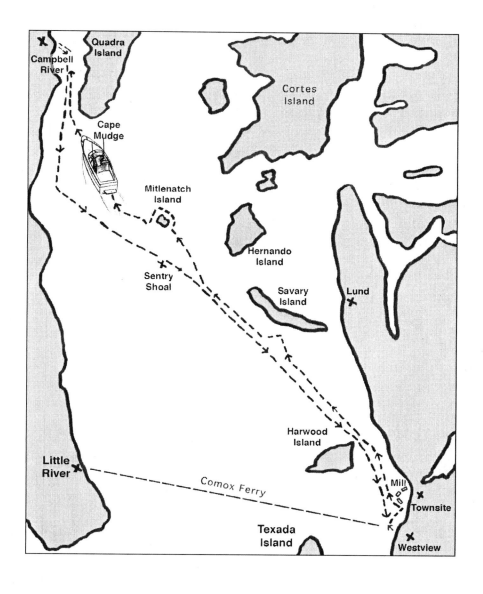

But a check of the GPS reveals that the smokestacks I see are not Campbell River, which lies farther north, out of sight behind the tip of Quadra Island. Instead, rising smoke past Cape Mudge pinpoints the city.

I readjust my heading for the cape, come up on-plane briefly, and then have to decelerate immediately to deal with yet another line of floating logs. Once again, we drift through a stagnant stretch of water. I use a quick burst of power, and then shift back into neutral to protect the prop. We don't make it all the way through, but another quick burst pushes us into the clean water on the other side.

A small fishing boat floats a kilometre to our left. It is a long, narrow canoe-like vessel, with a flat stern and a small outboard. The waves here are only a little over a foot high, but this small vessel is a long way from shore. I guess everything is relative when you possess experience and local knowledge of these waters.

A fast sport-fisher outboard crosses in front of us, headed towards Campbell River. He's moving at about 40 klicks, slapping the waves abruptly with his tough hull. This is another sign of experience, probably with a bit of desire to show off.

The sharp indentation of Discovery Harbour is clearly visible on the GPS. As we approach this area of intense nautical activity, rows of marinas pass along our left side. The Quadra Island ferry crosses in front of us, headed towards its Campbell River dock and verifying to me that the next opening in the breakwater is the fuel dock. I've been here before on a solo voyage around Quadra Island, and all looks familiar. The fuel dock is big and commercial-looking, using huge tires as dock fenders. There are no boats at the dock on this February afternoon, but as we approach, the fuel attendant immediately appears. He is probably surprised to see two people huddled on the command bridge of this relatively small vessel. We're obviously bundled for the cold, but we've elected to be exposed to the winter air. Rare winter tourists, to be sure.

I misjudge the approach, turning my bow away from the dock too soon. Shifting the motor into reverse doesn't kick the ass around in time, and we float parallel to the dock, over a metre away. Somehow the fuel attendant grabs a rail and pulls us against the dock.

"I bet you can tell we're amateurs," I yell to the attendant.

On this high dock, he is eyeball-level with me on the command bridge. He laughs.

"Of course, there hasn't been much chance for practice in recent weeks," I add, providing my favorite excuse for my lack of boating experience.

He smiles. It has been a rainy and windy winter, with few breaks for recreational boating. Today offers us all a glorious eight-hour stretch of sunny breaks in an otherwise savage season.

As I shut off the engine, Margy points to a large building adjacent to the fuel dock. *Superstore* it says in big blue lettering. I'm all for quiet and remote, but this sudden dose of city commerce catches my eye and makes me smile. Ma and Pa Kettle are comin' to town.

After gassing up, I move the Bayliner to the adjoining dock so it will be out of the way while we are at the store, and then Margy and I walk the short distance to the street.

I'm not sure what to expect (a single superstore, maybe), but the elaborate shopping mall is a distinct surprise. There are automobiles everywhere, with the shopping mall stores arranged in an L-shape. There are brand names we haven't seen in a long time and a variety of restaurants. We forgo our onboard lunch that sits in a paper bag back in the Bayliner, springing for the fish and chips. Then we wander the aisles of the Real Canadian Superstore, marveling at the huge inventory compared to the biggest stores in Powell River.

We purchase nothing, but make a mental note of how quickly we can get here in the Bayliner. We also remind ourselves of our shop-at-home attitude, which helps keep the local economy healthy. Powell River may not have a superstore, but everything you really need seems to eventually go "on sale" in town somewhere, if you wait long enough.

When we return to the fuel dock, a large fishing vessel is taking on diesel. The two crew members watch us walk to the Bayliner at the adjacent dock. They are probably surprised to see us climb up onto the command bridge and don our winter headgear. They're big and tough. We're little, but certainly not wimpy in the February open air of the upper deck.

The harbour is full of flotsam, so we motor out slowly, weaving between the biggest hunks of log. As we exit the breakwater, a tug appears off our bow about a 100 metres away, towing what looks like a complete city behind it. Well, it might not be a complete city, but it's at least part of a village – three wide-roofed structures nearly touching each other and riding high above the water on their own floating foundations. It's a logging or fish camp en route to a new location. If you don't like your town, its time to move, buildings included.

The weather has not yet turned sour, but there is now a different feel to the air. The sky to the south is threatening, and the air has a colder bite. As we proceed towards Cape Mudge, the waves grow to two-foot swells.

"Do you remember what time the ferry leaves Comox?" I ask Margy.

It would be nice to hold an escape plan handy; following the ferry across to Powell River is not a bad idea in rough conditions. Our speed on-plane is about the same as the *Queen of Burnaby's* steaming velocity. We could safely settle in a few hundred metres behind and let the ferry break the waves for us.

"Maybe it departs at 3:15, but I'm not sure whether that's the time for leaving Powell River or Comox," replies Margy.

We see the ferries come and go from Powell River all day long, but except for the first ferry of the day, we don't pay attention to the time.

"We could follow it across, if we need to," I suggest. "Of course, if the weather deteriorates, we could always spend the night in Campbell River or Comox."

True – but with the typical winter storm cycle, spending a night could mean spending a week.

I navigate south along the Vancouver Island coast towards Comox, but the waves grow rapidly larger, and the sky directly ahead of us is the darkest of all directions. After a few minutes of heading towards Comox, I decide crossing the Strait farther north might be wiser. So I turn the Bayliner left towards the tip of Savary.

"Looks brighter over there," I say. Margy is not surprised at my decision, and nods her head in agreement.

The conditions are within the comfort limits of the Bayliner, but just barely. We are pushing against southeasterly swells, with Mitlenatch off to our port side. Again the illusion of the island grabs our attention. It seems like forever before Mitlenatch moves behind us.

The wind has not switched to the northwest as forecast. It's evident that the next storm is already moving in. Regardless of the pounding waves, I stay on-plane as much as possible; it's best to get home quickly.

We hit a series of three-foot swells and increasingly gusty winds. My favorite USC hat flies off and disappears in the wake behind the Bayliner. It's not the first hat I've lost from the command bridge; usually I can turn around to retrieve a cap, but today I reluctantly elect to ignore it. Reversing course in these seas is not a pleasant prospect, and the heavy swells have probably swallowed my favorite hat anyway.

Lines of wood still challenge us, so I reduce to idle every few kilometres and drift through columns of floating logs. It's near low tide now, and I'm concerned about Grant and Mystery Reef, which lie ahead and to the right of our course. When I look for them on the GPS, I notice a familiar name even closer to our immediate right – Sentry Shoal. On the GPS screen, there is a plus sign at the west end of the shoal, indicating the marine weather buoy that broadcasts the sea conditions through good weather and bad. We are too far away to see the buoy, but it's exciting to be at this spot. Until this moment, I had no idea where Sentry Shoal was, but now I will pay closer attention to this ocean buoy's report when I hear it on the marine weather channel.

I aim for the smoke pouring out of the Powell River pulp mill stacks. The weather ahead looks brighter. Harwood Island's sand spit is easily visible now, and soon we should be in the island's leeward protection. It's not a very high island, but it will break up the swells coming up the strait from the south.

The Bayliner slips into the shelter behind Harwood, and the waves die back down, into our comfort zone. It's now a smooth ride the rest of the way home on a day that has served us with a wonderful respite from the winter weather – Sea Lion Day.

Chapter 7

Silver Streak

On the Powell River Books web page, a link allows readers to provide feedback regarding my books. I take readers' comments seriously.

An interesting feedback message arrives from Ken, a retired University of British Columbia professor from Gibsons. I respond via email, and the communication develops into an immediate friendship. There is something about Ken's message that identifies him as a unique resident of the BC coast. It takes a while for me to figure out the details.

After a series of email volleys, I visualize Ken as a bearded Canadian UBC professor and experienced boater. I imagine a pipe dangling from his lips, in the manner of a scholar and historian. My visualization turns out to be partly correct, except for the beard and pipe. I miss by a mile regarding his Canadian background (he is of American heritage), and his boating experience is relatively new, although particularly intense.

Ken describes his boat as a metal-hulled Silver Streak. The model name means nothing to me, but I imagine a rugged workboat design, capable of almost any sea conditions. Ken talks about Howe Sound and his cabin on Passage Island. He mentions some of his boating destinations well north of Desolation Sound. These are places I desire to visit, but it's debatable whether my Bayliner is big enough for such a challenge.

* * * * *

One blustery October day, I depart Powell River for Vancouver via Pacific Coastal Airlines, the first stop on the way to California. Originally, this flight was scheduled (a term used loosely) for my Piper Arrow, but the jet stream roars overhead, ushering in strong southeasterly winds and a torrential downpour. The Arrow is temporarily grounded in Powell River, in exchange for a safer ride on Pacific Coastal.

I have a lot of faith in Pacific Coastal pilots. Like most regional airlines, their pilots are young and enthusiastic. Young is fine with me, since I've worked with young pilots for three decades as an aeronautics instructor. Youth equates to quick thinking, superior reaction time, and overall excellence in the cockpit. But youth also equates to pushing the envelope and a lack of fear. I've noticed how tame my flight habits are today compared to the envelope I pushed in my early flying years. As they say: "There are old pilots, and there are bold pilots, but there are no old, bold pilots."

In fair weather, I rest comfortably in the cabin of a regional airliner. But it's not easy for a pilot with thousands of hours of flight experience to ride in the back seat of any airplane during rough weather. I am no exception. When it gets bumpy, I hang on tight and pray.

In stormy conditions, I imagine those young pilots in the cockpit pushing the envelope. There is a lot to be said for professional training and recent experience, and Pacific Coastal pilots have both. But the two pilots in the turboprop's cockpit generally have less total flight hours (combined) than I do. That can be a bit disconcerting in turbulent conditions. And I hate turbulence.

On the way to Vancouver on this mid-day flight, the twin-engine turboprop is tossed every which way. We are above the clouds, and that is good, but the descent into Vancouver is not a pleasant experience. I hang on tight as we enter the clouds. Just south of Bowen Island, we break out of the solid layer of overcast. Below us are scattered cumulus clouds and my first view of the ocean since leaving Powell River. The swells are huge, with whitecaps that are extensive and threatening. I try to imagine what it would be like to be in those waves, even in the largest boat. Under these conditions, our 24-foot Bayliner would be out of the question.

I motion to Margy, who sits behind me, pointing my hand towards the cabin window and the sea below. She understands immediately, and I hear her yell to me over the roar of the turboprops: "Wow!" is all she says. Like me, she is probably trying to imagine what it would be like aboard a boat in this savage sea.

That evening, back in California, I check my email. Among the messages is a short note from Ken. He ran into bad weather trying to take the Silver Streak home from Bowen Island at mid-day today, after an overnight stay with friends. As we descended above the ominous waves at the south end of Howe Sound, Ken was navigating his Silver Streak back to Gibsons nearly directly below us. Ken writes in his email: "I had checked the weather report on Bowen before we left, and I knew it would be ugly."

The Silver Streak must be a robust boat, and Ken is obviously a strong-minded boater. But it still leaves me in awe.

I reply to Ken immediately, telling him about my coincidentally simultaneous observations from the airliner high above Howe Sound. I remark how impressed I am with the capabilities of his boat, and he responds to my email with a photo attachment that shows the Silver Streak riding in a boat parade near Gibsons. It is a classic design and very attractive. But more impressive – it's a small (17-foot) welded aluminum boat with only a 75-horsepower outboard motor.

* * * * *

Ken has already been as far north as Echo Bay, opposite the northern tip of Vancouver Island. He dreams about taking his boat to Alaska. For years, I have imagined the challenge of taking my Bayliner that far. For me, it has been a questionable goal. Yet I am convinced Ken is indeed going to Alaska.

His boat has a tiny cabin with no galley or bed, and his gas supply is from two cruise-a-day portable tanks. Thus, driving in remote areas requires planning well in advance for gas and lodging, plus keeping a constant eye on the weather. Upon arrival at Minstrel Island, his wife Samantha (Sam) had to help with dishes in the hotel kitchen to convince the staff to feed them, exemplary of the challenges they would face on the way to distant Alaska in this small boat.

Ken is a U.S. economist who came to the University of British Columbia as a visiting professor and made it into a career. He acquired dual citizenship and retired in Gibsons a few years ago. While at UBC, he built a cabin on Passage Island and became an accidental boater.

"I needed a parking spot for my car near the water-taxi dock, and a boat slip came with it," explains Ken. "So it seemed logical to buy a boat."

Arrival on Passage Island is a particular challenge because there is no pier. Ken and his neighbors share a set of shoreline steps. They built a two-ton crane to heft their dinghies out of the water. The island's rocky shore is one of the reasons Ken selected the robust Silver Streak. Upon arrival at Passage Island, he carefully navigates his boat against the cliff-like steps. This necessitates a few whacks against his hull in all but the calmest conditions. At the shoreline, Sam exits (only possible at high tide), and Ken retreats to the mooring buoy. Then he launches his dinghy towards shore, where the small boat is hoisted up onto the dinghy dock. The dock's crane is a remarkable structure, but it's hard to visualize using this as a method of arrival at a modern, fully-equipped cabin.

Ken's attitudes are similar to mine, so it is not surprising we become immediate friends. On a visit to Powell River, we walk the docks together and inspect the Bayliner.

"So roomy," says Sam. "It seems really spacious compared to the Silver Streak."

Yet they're going to Alaska in the Silver Streak someday soon. Of that, I am convinced.

Sam is a Canadian who grew up in Ontario and moved around a lot, holding a variety of jobs in counseling. Eventually, this led to UBC and a later-in-life meeting with Ken.

While Ken taught at UBC, he responded to an inquiry by a cruise ship company seeking a guest professor as naturalist for an Alaskan cruise. They weren't looking for an economist, but Ken is able to talk about almost anything. So he applied for the position and was hired. His billing competed with another on-board guest speaker, Walter Cronkite of news broadcasting fame. Walter was well retired at the time, but still able to draw a large crowd at his presentation involving media coverage of world affairs.

When Ken arrived aboard the cruise ship, he was handed a nametag labeled *Naturalist*. Now that's a bit of a stretch. But Sam was at his side offering assistance from her broad knowledge about nature and the environment. During one slide presentation, she cringed while Ken pointed out whales in a photo speckled with a pod of Pacific white-sided dolphins. No one seemed to notice this incongruity of nature except Sam.

Ken is a great example of a transplanted American who has adapted perfectly to BC. Dealing with U.S. guests on this cruise was easy, since he clearly understands Americans. When passengers approached him (with his prominent *Naturalist* nametag), he always had an answer for them.

As they chugged past Campbell River, entering Johnstone Strait, one Texan was perplexed: "I'm still confused," he remarked. "Now which side is Canada, and which side is the United States?"

Better yet was the concern of a Georgia resident who said: "I just don't get it. Why do we have to go through Canada to get to Alaska?"

Knowing Ken, I'm certain his answers were polite but sprinkled with his unique sense of humor that is not understood by everyone.

* * * * *

After Ken and Sam visit us in Powell River, I want to visit Gibsons in the Bayliner. I've never been to Gibsons by boat, except for quick fuel stops to and from Vancouver. But I remember the open stretch of water south of Sechelt as daunting. For such a trip, the weather must cooperate. Even though it is now winter, I'd prefer not to wait until late spring or summer for the voyage, so I start monitoring the approaching weather systems for a guaranteed two-day break between storms.

Of course, there is no such thing as a guarantee at this time of year. A visit to Gibsons by Bayliner will need to wait for another season.

* * * * *

Before I am able to find an appropriate weather window to travel to Gibsons, Ken and Sam visit Powell River again. It is now June, and they are here to meet friends from the Gibsons Yacht Club. This small but active group of boaters travels together to Desolation Sound each year for an outing that lasts a full month. The group cruises primarily in sailboats, but Ken normally joins them for a few days in his Silver Streak. This year he is temporarily grounded while Sam recovers from a broken shoulder, suffered after being thrown from a horse. So they drive to Powell River to meet their friends from the yacht club.

Sam brings an edited copy of my soon-to-be-released (at the time) book, *Up the Winter Trail*, having accepted my request to edit the manuscript during her recovery from the horse accident. Ken warned me that Sam is the most thorough editor I'll ever meet. She uses her red pen on everything she reads, whether requested by an author or not. It's part of the method she uses to study the writing process on a regular basis. That's perfect for me, no matter how rigorous her editing may be. I'm quick to accept constructive criticism. That's partly because I easily disregard any recommended sentence restructuring I don't like, regardless of my grammatical errors. It's certainly not the most efficient way to handle the editing process, but it works for me. It also, admittedly, protects me from literary excellence as an author.

On today's ferry ride to Powell River, Sam finds a short article written by me in an onboard copy of *Powell River Living* magazine. She presents it to me, covered with red ink, including an edit of my two-sentence byline in *About the Contributors* at the front of the magazine.

Ken and Sam make a wonderful contrast. There is "The Ken Way," which I admire. It's an easy-going attitude that might be described as "good enough." It's coupled with a unique sense of humor that not everyone understands, but I do. Ken blasts ahead full-speed. Sam holds on tight and tries to throttle him back. But it's difficult to throttle Ken when he gets going.

Sam, on the other hand, has two speeds: anchored and full-speed ahead. In her editing, she's in the let-'er-rip mode, producing a blinding display of red ink. Ken calls it being "Samified." He describes "Samifying" as doing things to excess and fussing above and beyond the call of duty.

For example, when Sam ties up their boat, it is "Samified," and it takes Ken at least ten minutes to untie it. On a trip northbound in the Strait of Georgia, the Silver Streak was headed for Campbell River for a nice hotel and dinner to celebrate Sam's birthday. But ten kilometres from their destination, two lightning bolts struck the nearby shore, followed by the sound of fire trucks. When Ken's thoughts turned to the concept of being in an aluminum boat during a severe lightning storm, he elected to duck into a nearby marina for the night, where Sam tied up the boat for the overnight stay.

The birthday celebration was a bit less festive than planned, since their motel didn't have a restaurant. But there was a nearby store, so Sam's birthday dinner was hotdogs she had to cook. Meanwhile, during the stormy night, the Silver Streak's dock lines were so "Samified" that they ripped part of the dock loose. When Ken and Sam returned to the marina, part of the dock railing dangled from their boat. They were not invited back.

Up the Winter Trail is similarly "Samified," and it takes me a lot of time to filter through the red-pen commentary. However, what I find under the red deluge is valuable to my final editing process. I use a lot of what she provides. I also learn a lot about women's rights, am told what I should do to improve my writing (in detail), and discover that reviewing edited material can be entertainment in itself. I've been "Samified," and the book's final version is significantly improved because of it.

* * * * *

As I walk the docks of Powell River's South Harbour with Ken, I realize what a rich variety of boats ply the waters of coastal British Columbia. This is the working end of the harbour – mostly fishing boats and tugs, as well as transient parking for recreational craft. Docking space in Powell River is tight during summer, but the wharfinger somehow slips the Gibsonites into the South Harbour.

Fishing boats are now returning from their day out on the chuck. One particularly large, metal prawn boat slides effortlessly into its parking spot, with quick blasts of its engines and bow thrusters. Or could the boat's captain be using only the asymmetrical thrust of his honkin' twin-diesels? In either case, I wish I could navigate sideways like this in my Bayliner.

The Gibsons Yacht Club has eight boats here today, and Ken introduces me to their crews. We sit with Ken's friends, Klaus and Fran, aboard a 31-foot Uniflite powerboat from Gibsons. It was originally designed as a Vietnam-era gunboat, now renovated for recreational use. Previously a 40-knot vessel, it is now propelled by two small, fuel-efficient diesels, cruising in style at seven knots. Since I am used to on-plane speeds, I'll probably never be able to convert to the trawler lifestyle, but I envy their attitude.

I talk with Frank, as he sits in the stern of his slick 36-foot Hunter. It's almost as if he is waiting for visitors to walk past his boat so he can provide a quick lesson in sailing. Frank sits facing the dock, one arm draped over his outboard kicker. He looks like an advertisement for Yamaha.

"Is that motor your secret to beating all of these other sailboats?" I ask.

"Don't need this when I have the fastest boat under sail," he replies, leaning even closer towards the motor.

I know almost nothing about sailboats. Frank gives me his simplified explanation regarding how his skookum sailboat derives its speed by using its two sails in concert to capture the full power of the wind. This man is intense about sailing.

"It's like an airplane, with one wing in the water," he explains. "It's all aerodynamics." For a pilot like me, he speaks in terms I can understand.

We walk two berths down the dock, where another sailboat from Gibsons sits. This 32-foot boat has sailed to Australia and back, piloted by an experienced Gibson seaman, Gord, and his capable helmsman and wife, Marlene.

"Would you do it again?" I inquire. It is a question they must get asked repeatedly.

"Not in this boat," says Gord.

He isn't insulting the design, but this 32-footer is a small boat for such a long and challenging voyage. I try to imagine being on a sailboat in stormy waves in the middle of the Pacific Ocean. For an amateur boater like me, it's not a pleasant image. I glance at Marlene.

"If this boat goes to Australia again, I won't be on it," she adds.

She doesn't sound resentful, just realistic.

* * * * *

The summer comes and goes with so many other priorities that the trip to visit Ken and Sam in Gibsons is delayed even further. But someday soon, I'll anchor off Molly's Reach, site of the TV series *Beachcombers*. I'll also visit Passage Island (at high tide, of course). And someday, the Silver Streak and the Bayliner may go to Alaska together.

◊ ◊ ◊ ◊ ◊ ◊ ◊

Chapter 8

Under the Microscope

While reading *Passage to Juneau*, Jonathan Raban's story of his sailboat voyage from Seattle to Alaska, I am impressed with several things. First, he expertly merges historic data with his present day adventures; second, he uses a microscope.

When the author pulls his microscope out of its case to examine the contents of the local seawater, I entertain thoughts of my own investigation of microscopic creatures living below my boat. I have not looked through a microscope in decades – in fact, not since an undergraduate biology class. A microscope is not an instrument that has particularly intrigued my scientific mind. My infatuation with telescopes and astronomy never extended to the microscopic world, although I am now amazed that I could go through life ignoring this realm of nature. When I visualize Jonathan Raban's microscope coming out of its case to examine the tiny creatures within the local seawater, I am immediately hooked. But, like many of my other interests, it is an enthusiasm that is pushed to the back of my mind, awaiting ignition by some other event.

Later in the year, while visiting a friend on the Washington shore of the Strait of Juan de Fuca, I sit back and enjoy the conversation as it turns to science. Gary is a lot like me; he's enthralled with the world of science but never pursued a professional career in the field. He proudly gives me a tour of his mineralogy laboratory, which lies partially unpacked after his recent move to the Pacific Northwest. Gary shows me his extensive mineral collection and a long shelf of books on mineralogy. Then he pulls the plastic cover off his microscope.

It is a beautiful instrument, professional lab quality with stereoscopic binocular eyepieces to provide a spectacular view of Gary's prize specimens. It reminds me of the microscope in *Passage to Juneau*. I picture myself anchored in a remote bay, settling into the boat's cabin, and removing my microscope from its case. I visualize myself examining a slide prepared from a few drops of local seawater. Microscopic creatures of immense variety swim into view. Of course, I don't own a microscope.

I suspect that modern microscopes have come a long way since my college days. Look at what has occurred in telescopes in the last few decades. Surely, microscopes have experienced a similar dramatic evolution, rising astronomically (so to speak) in technology while simultaneously dropping in price.

A check on the Internet with the Google words *Microscope Discount* leads to web pages that confirm my suspicions. Microscopes for amateurs have definitely spiraled upward in technology and downward in cost. But it takes further research to understand the basics of modern microscopes.

The variety of instruments is daunting. Most of the newer scopes boast stereoscopic views and digital photographic capabilities. I soon learn that I need neither. In fact, these impressive microscopes are designed for the kind of work Gary does with minerals – stereoscopic, low-power magnification of solid objects. For what I want to do, examining tiny translucent specimens, a higher-powered compound (traditional) microscope is more appropriate.

I decide to let these ideas sit for awhile and purchase later. But, as usual, I can't wait. Within a few days, I have made an online purchase of a microscope, a beginner's slide kit, and two books about the microscopic world. I'll need to warn John that he will be receiving another package for me, since his home is my shipping address. Periodically, his house becomes crowded with packages awaiting my pickup. At the time I order the microscope, John is already expecting 800 copies of *Up the Main* and a reconditioned nose landing gear strut for my Piper Arrow.

The microscope I select is a compound binocular model (but not stereoscopic), with magnification up to 400-power and a "mechanical stage" for fine-tuning the slide's position under the lens using geared knobs. It uses a built-in light with rechargeable batteries for slide illumination, which seems ideal for the boating environment. I am surprised to find that modern microscopes have internal lighting, since I have only used old classroom models with a tiny mirror that must be oriented at a precise angle for an adequate view. Things have come a long way in forty years.

* * * * *

While waiting for the arrival of my microscope, I fiddle with the accessories that have already been received. I have slides and cover slips, storage trays, and a variety of tools, including an eyedropper and glass pipette. The packages continue to arrive at John's house, including more books on microscopes and microscopic organisms.

Since the microscope is delayed in shipment, I use the time to catch up with topics related to marine microbiology. My memory recharges quickly, even though my last view through a microscope was at the University of Buffalo in the late 1960s. One of my favorite publications is a children's book entitled *A World in a Drop of Water* (Alvin and Virginia Silverstein). It reintroduces me to microscopic critters I recall reading about decades ago, beginning with the ever-so-basic amoeba and the cilia-propelled paramecium. I read about stentors, spirogyra, rotifers, planaria, hydra, and my all-time favorite, the euglena. The euglena is the original, and still rare, animal-plant crossover species, with animal-like propulsion from a flagellum and self-contained plant-like chlorophyll.

I read about microbiology late into the night. With a flood of enthusiasm, I relearn the basics. Like riding a bicycle, you don't entirely forget how to find your way around the microscopic world.

I need some additional accessories to make my analysis of water samples complete. First, I'll require a specimen net, so I build one from the frame of a butterfly net I find mixed in with the fish nets at Canadian Tire. I sew one leg of a nylon stocking onto the net's circular frame and shove a plastic jar into the toe. I add an extended handle from an old broom that should keep the net far from the contaminated boat, dock, or shoreline when I retrieve my water samples.

I keep a related project clearly in focus. Powell Lake is notoriously deep, over 1000 feet in some locations. The lake was originally an oceanic fjord, carved out by an ice-age glacier 13,000 years ago. When the ice sheet retreated, sea water flowed in, and the basin became an ocean inlet. Over the next few thousand years the land rose, rebounding as the weight of the glacier lessened – "isostatic rise." About 10,000 years ago, the fjord was cut off from the ocean by the rising land, leaving landlocked Powell Lake. As fresh water flowed into the lake's northern inlet, salt water was pushed back into the ocean at the south end through a short outlet now called Powell River. But some of the saltwater (heavier than fresh water) sank to the bottom of the lake, where it has remained ever since.

What kind of microscopic critters now live in the trapped salt water at the bottom of Powell Lake? Professional marine biologists utilize expensive Niskin bottles to capture water from such depths, but maybe John and I can invent a simpler and cheaper method. This project is perfect for John's engineering skills, and my new microscope will stand ready to examine any microscopic life that might exist at the bottom of the lake.

* * * * *

Finally, the microscope arrives in a suspiciously battered box. Crossing the border from the States is a breath-holding ordeal for both people and packages. A hole in the side of the box reveals styrofoam packing inside the hacked cardboard. But the microscope inside seems protected and visibly intact.

A two-sheet parts list accompanies the instrument, but there are no instructions for using the microscope. A few paragraphs in the spec sheets include unillustrated steps for assembling the instrument from its four basic components.

I begin my microscopic exploration without the introductory instructions I expected with the microscope. Fortunately, I have a slide kit standing by (there is none in the package). I wonder how an enthusiastic youngster would react when opening such a gift on Christmas morning. As much as a child might try, there would be nothing to see without at least a slide, cover slip, and some basic instructions. Dad and a disappointed child would probably waste a lot of Christmas day trying to get something to happen, and it wouldn't.

But I am ready to go, except for the one tool that is needed to assemble the device. It is described in the minimal instructions as "a small screwdriver." I have two little screwdrivers in my backpack, one designed for the tiny screws used in eyeglasses. Neither is small enough to secure the eyepieces to the binocular attachment. The unsecured eyepieces won't fall out, but it would have been nice if the microscope's manufacturer had included an inexpensive version of the required miniature screwdriver. There are probably fewer amateur microbiologists in the world than I expected, and those few must be persistent in overcoming numerous consumer obstacles along the way. I wonder how many give up trying?

At my cabin during mid-December, I use the hand pump at the sink to extract my first water sample. The pump draws water from two metres deep, so it should not suffer any surface contamination. I pump for a few minutes to ensure there is no residue from the pipe. Then I collect a pan full of water and set it aside to settle. After a few hours, I use an eyedropper (not included with the microscope, of course) to extract water from near the bottom of the pan where microscopic critters would likely settle. This refined sample rests in a small plastic jar for two more hours. Then I draw a full eyedropper from the bottom of the jar and stand the dropper vertically so the microscopic organisms will accumulate at the glass tip.

This all sounds very scientific. In reality, my detailed procedure is extracted little by little from a variety of books I have accumulated. There is a lot written for amateurs regarding what you might find under high magnification, but almost nothing about how to prepare it for viewing in a microscope. So I invent my own method from a hodgepodge of hints gathered from the manuals.

I am now nearly ready for viewing. Using the eyedropper, I put a few small drops on a white plastic dish. The theory here is that the first drops will contain the densest residue from the lower end of the eyedropper, and each successive drop will be clearer. In case I am overwhelmed by the quantity of organisms, I can turn to the least clouded drop (last out of the dropper).

In the world of professional astronomical telescopes, what is about to happen is called "first light," the moment when a new telescope is turned skyward after the lengthy construction process. Standard astronomical objects are selected for viewing during first light, to allow a good evaluation of telescopic quality. It's an exciting moment for astronomers, since the capabilities of a new telescope are estimated rather than guaranteed. I enjoy the same sense of anticipation now, as my microscope is about to see first light.

I set the microscope on the kitchen table and spread my slides to the side. Lab journal sheets are standing by to record my observations and drawings of microscopic life. No drawing will be more significant to me than the first, regardless of the level of discovery.

My cabin's small kitchen has become a scientific laboratory. My always-ready Schmidt-Cassegrain telescope sits on a tripod next to the kitchen table and the new microscope; scientific instruments intermixed with kitchen utensils. From the microscopically tiny to the astronomically gigantic, I'm ready to explore whatever sized object comes my way.

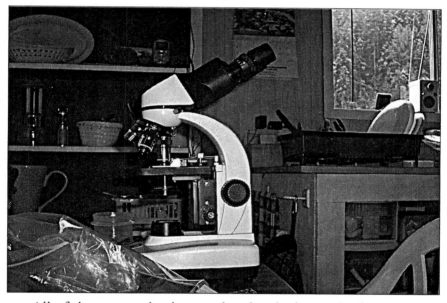

All of the water splotches on the plate look exactly the same, perfectly clear, so I select the first sample that should (in theory) contain the highest concentration of organisms. I transfer two drops of this sample to a slide and place a cover slip on top.

I try lowest magnification first. Using the 40-power lens, I move the knurled knob to focus on the sample. Objects are scattered throughout the field of view. Using the knobs for the mechanical stage, I pick the largest object and move it to the center of the field. I rotate the lens holder to the 100-power setting and center the object more precisely. Then, without refocusing, I skip right to maximum magnification of 400.

The object looks alive, but there is no movement. It is amoeba-like with gray to black structure and light brown zones. I think I see movement in a tentacle-like extension, but it stops immediately. Or is it a figment of my imagination? Whatever this is, alive or not, I am thrilled that I am seeing an object with such detailed structure.

Now I turn my attention to the rest of the water droplet. The fine movement controls of the mechanical stage are jerky. They push the slide up and to the left, but not down and to the right, so I keep pushing the slide back into position with my fingers. The stage movement problem is further frustrated by the complete lack of operating instructions to guide me. I fiddle with the diaphragm and condenser, making adjustments that are totally experimental. I'd like to try one of the color filters, but there are no instructions regarding how to install them. Writers of computer manuals deserve bragging rights over microscope manufacturers; but not by much.

I inspect the large amoeba-like object, sketching it on the first sheet of my lab journal. I add the examination conditions (magnification and sample information) that describe my "first light" observation. Whether alive or not, there is special significance to this first observation, and I'm thrilled by the occasion.

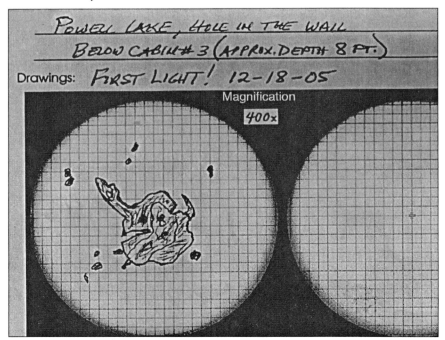

I prepare another slide. Maybe the gravity-settled droplets are too small to keep the organisms alive during my extensive settling process. I use the eyedropper to extract water from the bottom of the pan and let the water settle again in the eyedropper, this time only a few minutes. Then I prepare a new slide using this new sample and add a cover slip.

Under the microscope, I get similar results with this slide. I then prepare still another slide, this time with more drops of water to assure plenty of living space for the organisms. On this slide I observe a nearly transparent serpent-shaped structure that seems to possess a nucleus near one end; but still no movement. The serpent spreads across the entire field of view at 400-power magnification.

Overall, the results are exciting but inconclusive. Maybe the water at a lake depth of two metres is not ideal. Microscopic life may, in comparison, teem in surface water. That's what I'll try next.

* * * * *

The following morning, it begins to snow. The accumulation on the deck is minimal, but it causes me to reflect on the microscopic life I am seeking in the water. Do these organisms change depth during the change of seasons? The winter water coming out of the pump is so cold it numbs your fingers when you wash your hands.

The lake never freezes, regardless of the air temperature, and fish certainly remain here all year long. So my hypothesis is that microscopic life is similarly unaffected, although there may be a seasonal change regarding the depth where life resides. These tiny creatures may need to head downward, far downward, to survive in the winter. Maybe I am wasting my time looking for microscopic lake life near the surface in the winter.

A floating rubber duck-topped water thermometer bobs near the cabin's front deck, tethered to the transition float. The shivering duck registers a temperature slightly above freezing. (A turtle-topped thermometer later replaces it, after a miscalculated boat docking maneuver crushes the poor ducky.) But the theory I now prefer (totally unfounded) is that the surface water is the most likely location for microscopic life in this lake any time of year. My amateur microbiology books provide no hints on the subject.

I stand at the tip of the most distant dock at the cabin and use my specimen net to collect a surface sample. I swipe the nylon net back and forth for five minutes to maximize the number of organisms that will settle into the collection cup at the bottom of the netting. As the nylon net swirls over the surface, I visualize tiny critters rapidly accumulating in the plastic container.

Back in the cabin, I go through the settling process again, using the eyedropper to extract sample drops. I place extracted drops on the plastic plate and select the perfect looking drop. Actually, all of the drops look perfectly clear and exactly alike.

Under the microscope, I examine several slides and find elaborate structures similar to the ones seen the day before. Once again there is no obvious movement within the samples. One creature pivots in the water, but it seems pushed by flow within the drop, rather than self-propelled. I find several large threads of obvious plant life, exhibiting brown and blue-green coloration. But animal life is impossible to confirm. Nothing looks quite like the diagrams and photos from my books.

On a more positive note, I overcome the difficulties of the mechanical stage, mastering smooth movements of the slide by mounting it at the edges of the slide holder and its metal finger. I even manage to switch to a blue filter, and I become more proficient with the diaphragm and condenser settings. Still, I wonder if I will ever see definitive animal life with this microscope, unless in another season or another location. The chance of seeing anything life-like at the very bottom of the lake seems even more doubtful.

* * * * *

When nothing else works, ask John. While John is visiting my cabin to repair a starting problem on the tin boat's outboard motor, I set up the microscope and drag my net for a water sample. This time I skim closer to shore. My initial concern about avoiding contamination has now changed to an eager pursuit of spots in the lake where life seems most likely.

I prepare a slide sample and slip it under the lens, scanning it slowly for any sign of movement. Once again, interesting structures appear, and some include greenish-blue and reddish colors indicating life, but there is no movement. I conclude that I am viewing plants, not animals.

"Take a look," I say to John.

He settles into the kitchen chair, and I show him how to use the essential microscope controls – the fine focus knob, stage adjustment levers, and how to rotate the lenses into position.

"I've got a microscope at home," he says. "Pretty much a toy. Haven't used it in years."

As usual, he quickly adapts to the technology and begins to scan the slide at medium magnification.

"There's something moving," he says.

John has been at the microscope only a few seconds, compared with the hours I've spent in close inspection. I'm suspicious.

"Could be an air bubble or a floater in your eye," I reply. "Air bubbles are perfectly round. You can try closing an eye to see if it's a floater." I watch John as he closes one eye and then the other.

"No, it's definitely alive. It's moving like crazy. Take a look."

I quickly change positions with him, and even before I can adjust the focus for my eyes, a transparent green worm-like object drifts across the field of view. It attaches itself to a piece of microscopic brown debris that looks (under magnification) like a giant decayed log. The organism crawls in and out of crevices in the debris and moves all over the place. I'm not sure what it is, but it appears to be a multi-celled organism. And it's alive!

We spend another half-hour inspecting the remainder of the slide, and John finds another smaller creature, gyrating wildly across the field of view. This looks like a single-celled animal, a lot like the rotifer I've seen in my microscope books.

I've searched for microscopic animal life in the water for many hours, and John finds it on his first try – in a matter of seconds. I should have known.

I now have a microscope to inspect water samples, and I've finally seen animal life. Now I crave a good look at a sample from the bottom of Powell Lake. I still don't have a deep-water probe or a way to get it into position at the bottom of the lake. But I do have determination.

◊ ◊ ◊ ◊ ◊ ◊

Gemini Launch at Mowat Bay: Ed, Helen, John, and Bro

Cabin Number 3, Hole in Wall, Powell Lake

Kemmerer Bottle Drop Near Three-Mile Bay, Powell Lake

Suzuki on Trail near Chippewa Bay: John and Margy

South Harbour, Westview Marina

Coast Guard *Cape Caution:* North Harbour, Westview Marina

John near Confederation Lake

Author Interviewing Bro in Theodosia Valley

Queen of Burnaby Approaching Westview Ferry Terminal

Bayliner at Cabin Number 3, Hole in the Wall

Savary Island from Bayliner Command Bridge

Outboard in a Barrel: John and Rick

Mr. Kayak at Lang Bay

Head of Jervis Inlet: Photo by John Maithus

Pender Harbour from Piper Arrow

Bro on Powell Lake

Bob's Crew Boat at Cabin Number 3: Bob, John, and Margy

John and Bro on Bayliner's Command Bridge

Chapter 9

Summer into Fall on Cortes

September has passed the halfway point, and it is a wondrous time on the chuck. The summer cruisers have disappeared to the south, except for those like us who take advantage of the shorter days, cooler nights, and slower pace.

The Bayliner slides into the fuel dock at Lund, with no attendant in sight. I ring the bell and wait, while Margy goes up the ramp for ice cream. She returns to the boat after the fuel attendant arrives and the Bayliner's main and auxiliary fuel tanks are pumped full.

"That took a while," I say, knowing that Margy's trip ashore has not gone as planned.

"Closed," she says.

Margy holds two pizza slices from farther up the road at Nancy's Bakery. It doesn't make sense that the dockside ice cream shop is closed on a warm afternoon during September.

"That shop has been in business only two months," I remark critically. "You'd think they'd want customers."

It always amazes me how many coastal BC shops set their own hours, seemingly oblivious to their clientele. My tendency is to not return to a place that keeps irregular hours, not wasting time wondering if they will be open. Local customers seem more accepting of this and grudgingly put up with the inconsistent schedules.

"Summer's over," proclaims Margy.

It's a contradictory truth, as evidenced by the afternoon sunlight beaming down onto the warm sea.

* * * * *

"**T**enedos should be nearly empty today," I predict as we motor out of Lund Harbour.

It's impossible to forget last summer's odyssey at Tenedos Bay. A bumbled anchoring exercise on a crowded day caused us to make a hasty retreat, embellished by a few expletives from me. I swore (undoubtedly more than once) I'd never go there again. But it's late September now, and we should have the bay nearly to ourselves.

We continue up Thulin Passage and around Sarah Point, entering Tenedos Bay with every expectation of having a more pleasant experience than our mid-summer incident. Only three boats are in Tenedos today. One sailboat is anchored in the scenic east cove. From there, it is a quick dinghy ride and short walk to Unwin Lake, a hike that tops the list of reasons why we have decided to visit Tenedos again. There's plenty of room for another boat in the east cove, but it's not a good spot for anything other than a day hook. With these northwest winds, a better place to drop anchor is the north corner of the bay, and only one boat occupies that extensive area. From there, it will be a short dinghy ride to the east cove and Unwin Lake.

We pull close to shore in the north corner, looking for a spot that suits us. But the GPS shows the depth at over 60 feet, except in places so close to shore that a stern line is required. I've experienced more than a few stern line disasters, none worse than here last summer. Today, swinging on the anchor is the only acceptable choice.

I try dropping the anchor at two different locations that seem marginally acceptable based on their shallow depth; mere knolls in the seafloor. In both spots, the anchor fails to grab, and we drift into deeper water. Remembering my summer problems, I'm hair-triggered for troubles in this bay, with a bad attitude that can lead to a self-fulfilled prophesy.

There is another place to try, but I feel my negative attitude battling my usual optimism. A pocket anchorage back near the bay's entrance could shelter our boat.

I maneuver the Bayliner around the rocky point near the entrance, and the anchorage blossoms into a scenic cove. The depth sounder confirms that this location is adequate. It is just a matter of positioning the boat near the center of the cove, to swing on a fairly short rode. The protection of the rocky point of land makes a long rope (large scope) unnecessary, but getting the anchor to hold has to be conquered first.

I stand on the bow and lower the anchor. When I feel the bottom, I signal to Margy on the command bridge. She shifts into reverse and backs away, as I let out a little more rope and then secure it to the windlass. We wait for the anchor to grab, but it doesn't. We try again, and again; three attempts get us nowhere.

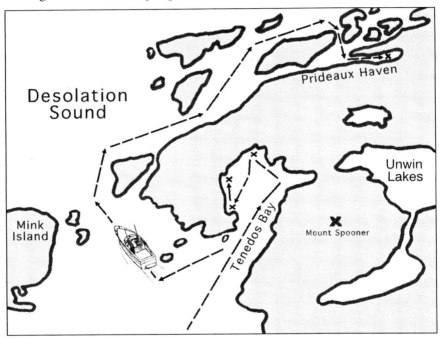

There's one other place I'm (barely) willing to try. The shallow entrance to Three Fathom Cove (west side of the bay) seems a reasonable place to anchor. The cove itself won't work due to the low tide expected in the morning, preventing any exit until near noon. But outside the cove's entrance seems to be an acceptable location.

With the boat positioned outside the entrance, I stand beside the anchor on the bow and glance back at Margy on the command bridge. I flash a big grin that I'm sure she'll correctly interpret as a false smile. She sees right through, as evidenced by the way she raises her eyebrows and says: "Good luck. – you'll need it."

I drop the anchor at a spot that should be not-too-deep. Then I motion to the command bridge. Margy backs, and backs, and backs. The anchor fails to grab.

"That's it! I'm finished here!" I yell to anyone within shouting distance (only Margy).

I give Margy my "halt" hand signal. It's time to raise the anchor for the sixth time today and get out of here. Far from cheery, I activate the foot switch for the winch, and begin to raise the anchor. The winch struggles for a moment and then pulls smoothly. An ugly, shredded yellow rope comes to the surface, wound around the anchor.

Now what? This looks like a rope of the type used as a stern line, probably abandoned by another disgusted boater. I dislodge the yellow line from the anchor, but it wouldn't be appropriate to throw it back overboard where it could foul another anchor or (worse yet) a prop. So I begin to haul the algae-covered rope aboard the Bayliner. I pull and pull and then it becomes taut. The line now appears to be a light anchor rode, probably still attached to an anchor that is lodged firmly on the bottom. I tug on the line, attempting to break it loose. It doesn't budge. There is only one reasonable solution.

I cut the rope as far below the surface as I can reach and then haul the filthy remnants onto the bow. The shredded yellow rope lies in a mucky pool on the forward deck, an ugly souvenir from Tenedos Bay.

There will be no Tenedos Trilogy. I ain't comin' back.

But what about a place to anchor today? I need a location that brings back pleasant thoughts. Maybe I can harness those memories to change my attitude, using mind over matter to get the anchor down. Prideaux Haven is the obvious choice, and it's nearby.

When I calmly suggest Prideaux, Margy immediately agrees. She is probably amazed I have survived six attempts to drop anchor today, and yet seem to have mentally cooled off already. I'm not typically such an easy-going guy, but thoughts of Prideaux Haven sooth me.

* * * * *

Prideaux holds only a few boats. Once inside, I aim for Melanie Cove, which is always packed in summer. On this mid-September day, the cove is nearly empty. We slip in, hugging the north shore to avoid the reef that looms along the other side at low tide. Two anchored boats sit a comfortable distance apart, sharing the normally crowded east end of the cove. I pull around them and begin what I hope is my last anchoring exercise of the day.

Even in this ideal depth (30 feet) with a near perfect bottom (mud), the anchor again refuses to hold. I retrieve it for another try, and still another. I pull the anchor back onto the bow and closely examine it. Could there be something wrong with my equipment? What can go wrong with a simple metal hook? Answer: It is not the anchor – it's just one of those days. Or maybe it's me.

"What's going on?" I yell back to Margy from the bow.

"Maybe it's the jellyfish," she replies. She sits at the helm on the command bridge, looking down at a very tired me.

I don't laugh at the jellyfish theory, because it's as good an answer as any. In fact, jellyfish are everywhere – large, transparent, and hovering just below the surface. There's no way they are to blame, is there?

I lower the anchor again; and again the backward movement of the boat refuses to set the anchor. This is never going to end.

Okay – there's absolutely no wind here now, we sit in a well-protected cove, and the forecast is for a calm evening. Under such conditions, boats can stay put with the mere weight of an anchor, without the hook embedded in the bottom, so I give in to the temptation. *Halcyon Days* floats on an anchor that's not lodged in the mud. It's pretty much a day hook on a short rode, but I get away with it.

I'm worn out. Lowering the anchor is a gravity-assisted operation, requiring a little muscle to control the drop. The electric winch handles the retrieval, but even during this procedure, some physical effort is necessary. After ten attempts today, I'm exhausted. I'm so tired that I don't want to deal with the barbecue. Lifting it from the boat's cabin to the rail of aft deck seems like an Olympic challenge, and there have been enough challenges in the last few hours. Thank goodness for the cold pizza. It tastes wonderful.

High tide arrives soon after sunset, with herring popping out of the water everywhere. As far as the eye can see, the tiny fish jump, plopping down with a splash. I remember the last time I saw this phenomenon. It too was near sunset at high tide, but in Bute Inlet, where I caught my first salmon within minutes after the herring surfaced. Could salmon be running through this cove tonight?

Quickly, I drop my fishing line into the water. The lure sinks almost immediately to the shallow bottom. I jig a few minutes before I remember that I'm in a marine park. Is fishing allowed here? I quickly retrieve my line and scan the two nearby boats to see if anyone is eyeballing me. It's probably an unfounded concern, but I put my fishing rod away.

* * * * *

The next morning, with the anchor still holding nicely as dead weight, herring repeat their leaping maneuvers. Larger splashes near the far shoreline look like salmon jumping. The salmon turn into porpoises, and then whales – in Melanie Cove?

These are large creatures coming completely out of the water, feeding and flopping with loud slaps on the calm surface. Binoculars solve the puzzle: seals are feeding in the early morning light. In their enthusiasm, they come fully out of the water. I have never seen seals this active. Now seals surround the boat. Are these the same seals covering a large territory, or is this a different bunch?

After raising anchor, we slowly motor out of Melanie Cove and Prideaux Haven. I navigate along the east edge of Eveleigh Island. It was along this entrance to Prideaux that Halcyon Days scraped her hull on these infamous rocks during a previous visit (*Up the Lake*, Chapter 16). Now it is near low tide, and the rock ledge that whacked us last year is clearly visible. The prominent rocks are a reminder that tight spots are often better navigated at low tide. When the water is low, you can more easily see obstacles that are normally submerged and invisible, but ready to cause damage.

Margy drives the Bayliner, bringing the boat up onto plane. I turn and look behind us, snapping a photo of the wake and mountainous scenery to the north. When I click the shutter, the framed image seems like an ideal cover photograph for this book.

My enthusiasm for what is seen in the viewfinder often turns to disappointment, since few photos capture scenes in a way that gives justice to the moment. It's proof that the eye and brain are the best recorders of beauty in the universe.

The photo portrays a curving path away from Prideaux Haven, with cloud-capped mountains and a bright blue sky in the background. The picture doesn't make it onto the cover of the book, but it does find its way into this chapter.

We haven't yet decided on today's destination. Our bicycles are aboard, so Margy and I discuss where to anchor for a bike ride. The previous summer, we attempted to explore Cortes Island on foot. That journey was cut short after the first mile of grunting uphill along the road as it leaves Cortes Bay. But bikes should work nicely, once past the hill. The government dock is an ideal location to off-load.

On our previous visit, we tied up to the dock for the night, in spite of our preference for swinging on-anchor. On that warm summer evening, an orange catamaran sailboat, *Hot Sauce*, pulled into the bay and swung pointedly toward the dock.

The boat's first pass was in preparation for its final approach, and I watched in amazement as the young crew nimbly maneuvered the vessel towards the dock. Sails full of wind, the catamaran swung by *Halcyon Days*, surveying the only available docking location, a tight spot right in front of us. *Hot Sauce's* captain, looking like a young yacht club Yuppie, stood firmly on the deck, his raised hand clutching the mast netting. As the impressive sailboat slid past us, the young captain politely yelled over his shoulder to us: "Would you mind pulling your dinghy out of the way?"

"Sure!" I hollered back. "Glad to help."

Mr. Bathtub bobbed next to our starboard side, and it was easy to quickly untie the lines and pull the dinghy behind the stern. The broad catamaran was preparing to parallel-park in a space that looked too tight for even a much smaller powerboat. Yet, *Hot Sauce* was making its docking approach under full sail.

The second pass (final approach) was a sight to behold. The young captain's sweater was draped around his neck, streaming behind him, an image right out of a yachting magazine. He yelled commands (noticeably polite) to his youthful crew. The helmsman (student pilot?) swung the catamaran's large wheel in a wide sweep as *Hot Sauce* skimmed within a metre of *Halcyon Days*, precisely through the water where our dinghy rested a few minutes before.

More brisk commands streamed from the captain, and *Hot Sauce* somehow thrust herself nearly sideways into the parallel parking berth, bumping gently against the rail of the dock. More swift commands from the captain, and the sails immediately collapsed. The tying of lines that quickly followed was itself a marvel of teamwork. *Hot Sauce* now sat in front of us, at full stop, the transom proudly displaying her home port: *Vancouver Yacht Club.*

* * * * *

Today we approach Cortes Bay, intending to offload our bikes at the government dock and then anchor nearby. The entry to the bay is deceptive; I don't see the entrance until we are on top of it. The red cement beacon finally appears, sitting near the middle of the channel.

The opening to the right of the beacon is wider, but the light announces red-right-returning: keep the beacon to the boat's starboard side when entering the bay. Inspection of the chart indicates a substantial reef to the right. I plan a course midway between the red light and the cliffs to the left.

As the government dock comes into view, binoculars reveal an inviting parking spot near the end, just inside the floatplane loading area. It is an ideal bike offload location. The more I think about it, the better I feel about using the dock for overnight moorage. Moving *Halcyon Days* in and out of the dock to deliver and retrieve the bikes is more of an inconvenience than a problem, but my lazy side is quick to surface. Besides, I haven't forgotten yesterday's anchoring follies.

Assisting in the decision is the arrival of a motorcycle nearly simultaneous with our arrival at the dock. As we tie up the boat, the slim rider parks the bike at the dock's entrance and walks down the ramp, blue helmet still on and clipboard in-hand. The helmeted figure strides along the dock, looking over the boats and noting information on the clipboard. It's now obvious that we have the opportunity to log ourselves in with the wharfinger for an overnight stay. It's like arriving at a fuel dock with the dock assistant holding a fuel nozzle. It's simply too inviting to resist.

"Good timing," I say to the still-helmeted motorcyclist. Now I can see it is a woman behind the partially raised plastic visor. "Can we pay our overnight fee to you?"

"Sure," she replies. "Or you can just leave your money in the honor box near the ramp."

"We'll pay you, if that's okay. We'll be here one night."

"How long?" she asks, nodding toward the Bayliner. She's referring to the length of the Bayliner, the standard for computing overnight fees.

"Twenty-four feet," I reply. The helmeted woman consults a tattered paper lodged near the bottom of her clipboard.

"Need electrical?" she asks.

"No, just dock space for the night," I reply.

"Looks like twelve-oh-seven," she reads from her clipboard. I dig out the exact change – $12.07. Nice round number.

"I got a bit nervous when I saw you," I admit. "I was expecting last summer's wharfinger." The normal wharfinger was in his late 80s when I last saw him, and I'm worried when I see he is not the one to greet us.

"Oh, he's fine," she laughs. "Some health issues, but I'm just filling in for him today. Everybody accuses me of stealing his job."

I offer a smile, and she nods in understanding. The jolly wharfinger of the previous summer is a legend in this area. He lives in the small house near the dock and is probably enjoying his rare day off.

"Could you give us some advice about biking around here?" I ask. "We want to ride to Manson's Landing, but I can't figure out the roads on the map. We'd like to avoid the hills?"

"That's hard to do on this island," replies the woman, helmet visor now fully lifted and protruding forward. "You can turn left from the dock entry road. That puts you on Bartholomew, and it'll take you all the way. It's a bit hilly at first, but it gets better after the first kilometre."

"How far altogether?" I ask.

She glances at our bicycles on the boat's aft deck, probably wondering if we know what we're getting into.

"Four kilometres to Manson's," she replies.

We discuss the route a bit more, asking about a way to make the return trip by looping around Hague Lake and back along Seaford Road.

"Not recommended," she says. "Unless you want to see some of our bigger hills."

I'm sure that anything considered particularly hilly by her is far beyond our biking abilities. We'll stick to Bartholomew Road.

* * * * *

Before we offload our bikes, I stroll towards shore to inspect a hefty fishing boat on the other side of the dock. I pace off the length of *Westview No. 1* – 90 feet. All of the boats at the government dock on this mid-September day are hefty workboats, except for us. That's the kind of dock I like, and it's the kind of dock you find most places in BC during the off-season.

With the bikes now sitting on the dock, I'm ready to lock the door of the Bayliner. But first I consult Margy: "Anything we might have forgotten?"

Margy understands. We have an ingrained habit of forgetting something we need when leaving for a hike or bike ride. I'm intent on developing a hiking-and-biking checklist, but I haven't done so yet.

"Can't think of anything," replies Margy. I lock the door, but before the key is in my pocket, she adds: "What about the batteries?"

"Oops, you're right."

I struggle with the aft deck engine compartment latch, trying to open it from the door well, not easy now that the cabin door behind me is locked. Finally, I get the hatch open, awkwardly get hold of the battery switch, and move it from *BOTH* to *# 1* for our overnight stay. It's a wise procedure that prevents complete electrical drawdown during an overnight stay.

"Anything else?" I say accusingly, as if Margy is to blame for my forgetting the battery switch.

"Not yet," she retorts. In other words, we'll finally realize it only when it happens, and it will.

As I step off the aft deck onto the dock, I notice Margy's camera, sitting outside of its case, balanced precipitously on the gunnel.

"Do you want this?" I ask.

"Oops. We do need a checklist," answers Margy, as I hand her the camera.

It's a tough push up the ramp, low tide making gravity our temporary enemy. At the first level spot above the ramp, we stop to check tire pressure. I use the opportunity to inflate one of my slightly soft tires.

"Do you know what we forgot?" asks Margy with a lilt in her voice, as I pump up my tire.

"Don't tell me," I answer sarcastically. "Whatever it is, we ain't going back."

I wait for Margy to respond, but she remains silent, putting the ball in my court. Of course, I want to know what we forgot.

"Okay, what did we forget?" I ask.

"Our helmets," she states curtly. We specifically loaded the bike helmets in a small bag for our dockside rides, and this is the second time in a row that we've left them behind.

"We're not going back," I reiterate.

* * * * *

It's a hilly ride to Manson's Landing, but only a minor challenge. Some of the hills we must walk, but most can be climbed in low gear. I have the advantage of greater momentum downhill because of my weight, plus I pull out all stops and coast freely or even pedal on the descents. Margy, on the other hand, uses her brakes going downhill, so she loses the gravity assist on the next uphill thrust. She isn't the most comfortable biker, but her determination makes up for her lack of skill. There isn't a hill she is unwillingly to scale on foot.

Since today is the Friday Market, all of the traffic (which is minimal) is headed towards Manson's Landing (technically Manson's Village, with the landing another kilometre beyond). Old pickups, several of them carrying homemade wheelbarrows, clatter past us. We encounter a few vehicles going the other way, returning from the market with full truck beds.

The uphill grades are beginning to take their toll on us, so we pause for a break at the only stop sign we've seen so far. Margy snaps a photo of me at the corner, under a street sign that reads *Salmonberry Lane*.

The next major junction is a T-intersection. It's decision time. I'm not sure whether Manson's Landing is to the left or to the right. We pause at the crossroads to ask directions from the next arriving vehicle.

A truck arrives from the left, and it turns onto the road we're exiting. I wave to the driver, thinking he will stop at my gesture. He responds with a friendly wave and barrels on through the intersection, disappearing down the road. Wrong kind of wave.

My next wave is to a well-rusted Volkswagen van (60s-style) that arrives at the intersection from the road behind us. This time my hand motion is more of a halt sign than a *Hello*. The van comes to a stop, and a smiling woman rolls down the passenger window.

"Which way to town?" I ask.

The passenger remains silent, while the male driver leans across her and responds: "Town right, beach left. It's not much of a town."

We turn right, and within a kilometre we arrive at another intersection. The Friday Market is inside the community center building to the left, and a few touristy shops and a cafe sit to the right. This is not tourist season.

We stop at the cafe, lock our bikes (probably unnecessary), and become the only customers at the cafe. We place our order for sandwiches and pop, and I beg a piece of paper and pen from the waitress, since I've forgotten my author's notepad (another checklist item).

"What's the best route to Hague Lake?" I ask the waitress.

"Right down the road on your right. You can't miss it. You'll see the public beach, just off the road to your right."

She says "public beach" with an emphasis that seems strange. I then remember what I have read about Hague Lake. There is a nude bathing area near the public beach, and this waitress is not sure what we are asking. So she takes the safe approach.

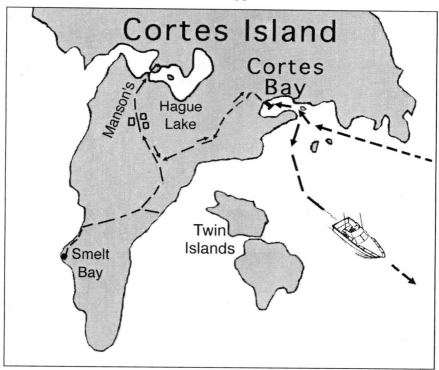

The Friday Market across the street is a busy place. Some of the traffic is routine business at the town's post office, located inside the community center. Downstairs, the market consists of a series of tables, some touting items that are clearly for tourists (postcards and jewelry), but we are the only tourons. Like many of the locals, homemade raspberry ice cream is what we go for, and it is as good as any I've ever tasted. There are produce tables too, and that is what the locals are most interested in.

Leaving the tiny village, we pedal towards Hague Lake. In less than a klick, we find a cutoff to the right. It's a narrow path that is blocked to motor vehicles by boulders, but our bikes pass through easily. At first, I think this path is taking us to the lake, but I soon realize it is a shortcut that curves around the next intersection. We rejoin the road at a downhill stretch that continues for at least another half kilometre.

"Let's leave our bikes here," I suggest. "Otherwise, it will be tough pedaling back uphill."

Margy is keen on avoiding uphill grades too, so we lock our bikes to a small tree, and hike down the hill. The turnoff to the public beach is clearly marked, but we want to visit the nude beach. We continue down the road and take the turnoff just before the creek that empties into Manson's Lagoon (and Manson's Landing). An unmarked parking area sits to the right side of the road. It looks like the beginning of a trail to the lake.

A short hike brings us to easily climbed rock cliffs overlooking the lake. A few heads pop up from nooks among the boulders, local bathers wondering who is approaching. We sneak in as silently as possible, trying not to intrude on their privacy.

The small lake is particularly scenic from this spot. We swim in comfortably warm water with a pleasant sandy bottom. It's a refreshing oasis after a bike ride on a mild September day.

* * * * *

Since there was more uphill than down on the trek from the Cortes dock, I expect the ride will be easier going back to the boat. And it does seem both easier and quicker.

After awhile, I slip behind Margy to assure I'm not setting too fast a pace. I watch her coast down a long incline, her brakes partially engaged and squeaking. As she walks the uphill stretch that follows, my momentum propels me past her until the climb gets too steep. Then I too am off my bike and walking to the crest, where I wait for her.

After the next downslope, as I watch from behind Margy, she slows to a crawl on the uphill climb that follows. Almost stopped, she steps to the ground. Suddenly, she plops to the pavement, her bike suspended motionless for a few seconds. Then her bike falls to the pavement beside her. It isn't much of a fall for either Margy or her bike at nearly zero forward velocity, but it looks odd.

"What happened?" I ask, as I pedal up beside her.

She slowly extracts herself from her flat-on-the-pavement position, while I pull her bike upright.

"My shoelace got caught in the pedal, and I fell as I was getting off the bike. But I'm okay."

"Quite a sight," I note. "Usually people don't fall off bikes when they're standing still."

"I try to do things differently," she laughs.

Without complaint, she begins to push her bike the rest of the way up the hill. I walk beside her to make sure she isn't hurt, and then we both start down the next hill together. I zoom ahead and am able to reach the following crest by coasting. As I pedal the last few metres to the top of the hill, I overtake a couple walking in the middle of the road. They retreat to the shoulder as they hear me coming. I pass them only slightly faster than they are walking.

"Careful," I yell over my shoulder as I pass. "There's a woman on a bike behind me, and she'll pass you at about 50 klicks."

"We'll be looking for her," replies the man.

(Margy later reports she almost caught up with the couple as she approached the turnoff to the dock. Then she got off her bike and walked a few metres behind them until she turned onto the road to the dock. I bet the couple wondered if this bicyclist, walking slowly behind them, was the 50-klick woman.)

I make the turn onto the road to the dock, slow a bit at the ramp entrance, and then brake more heavily as my bike slips down the less-inclined (at higher tide) ramp. My brakes squeak severely, but there is no one to hear. I glide past *Westview No. I,* and roll to a stop on the dock beside the Bayliner.

September, bikes, and islands. It's a good combination. Bring a camera, and don't forget your helmet.

◊ ◊ ◊ ◊ ◊ ◊ ◊

Chapter 10

Gemini II

With the refurbishment of *Gemini* in full swing, John is on a work schedule that moves the structural modifications towards completion. While I am in California, the rear deck starts to take shape, and the aft cabin wall is rebuilt. In his zeal to increase interior space for my writer's retreat, John tears out the wall that separates the head from the cabin. Originally we had decided to use this space for shelves, but now it is usable as floor space. I tell John I concur, even though he has already announced that the teardown is complete. It's a good thing John makes decisions that suit me.

Upon return from the States, Margy and I join John during one of his scheduled workdays in the hangar. We're good grunt workers, and I'm glad we can relieve him of some labor.

I climb under the boat and begin the dirty job of wet sanding the bottom of the hull. A filthy mixture of flat-black bottom paint, water, and dead barnacles slops all over me.

John's electrical grinder emits a piercing shrill as he scrapes away old epoxy patches on the hull. He pulls off the transom's kicker mount and the deteriorated swim grid, and plugs holes left behind after the removal of equipment that no longer requires hoses, cables, and wiring. The scupper drain from the old sink is filled, as are a variety of dings and deteriorated fiberglass patches.

In the hangar, *Gemini* sits next to *Mr. Float Cabin*, a bookmobile on a utility trailer that sports a hot dog cart design. Soon *Mr. Float Cabin* will be pulled through the streets of Powell River, hopefully turning heads as it passes. ("Hey, Joe, look at that thing? – it looks like a float cabin on wheels.")

Today, the hangar holds *Gemini*, two quads on a trailer, Mr. Float Cabin, and the Campion's empty boat trailer. There is no room for the hangar's primary occupant, my Piper Arrow, so the airplane sits in an outside tie-down spot next to the Westview Flying Club's Cessna 172. If all goes well, *Gemini* will be in Powell Lake before the first winter storm, and the Arrow will be back under cover.

* * * * *

At the end of a Sunday at the hangar, I lock the airport gate while John leaves. I roll down the hill from the airport, John leading in his truck by a half-kilometre When I reach the carpet store on Duncan Street, John is parked in front, standing by a pile of old carpet, and waving me in.

I pull up next to him and roll down my window. John points to the pile of carpet that lies against the building.

"Just what you need," he says. "It'll work perfect in *Gemini*."

"Let's load it up," I say.

It's late Sunday afternoon, and the carpet store is closed. John laughs and shakes his head: *No.*

"Do you think it's just discarded?" I ask.

"Could be, or maybe they just left it outside because it's not the good stuff. But it would look fine in *Gemini.*"

"I'll check with them tomorrow," I say, although I'd probably prefer a newer looking piece of carpet.

We've just finished surveying the interior of the old boat at the hangar, talking about paint and carpet. This project is finally starting to look like something very special, thanks to John's hard work and his expert renovations. Of course, I've contributed some of my own ideas. But mostly, I just let John go in whatever direction he feels comfortable. Every day, *Gemini* is looking more like a writer's floating retreat.

Working with John is both enjoyable and agonizing. His production standards are so high that I am unable to perform even the simplest task without worrying he will make me redo it to meet his high standards.

One day, without John's probing eyes present, I cover the above-waterline hull with its third (and final!) coat of signal-red marine paint. John inspects the surface the next day, running his hand down the side of the boat.

"Rough," he says. "Looks like your roller was crappy, and you painted over some bugs that got stuck in the previous coat."

"Good enough," I reply, with an intentionally disgruntled tone.

"You can smooth those spots with steel wool, and then apply another coat."

"No way. That's the last coat." I'm finished with the red paint, and I plan to stick to my guns.

"You don't want to leave it like that," states John.

"But I do want to leave it like that. You can't see those spots, and who is going to run their hand along the hull? It's good enough."

"But we'll know it's there," replies John.

This is one of John's often-repeated phrases when defending his stringent work standards. He even used it on me after inspecting a scratch in the flat-black bottom paint, the coating intended to protect the underwater portion of the hull. Since this scratch was below the water line, I tried not to give in: "It's underwater, John. You can't even see it. Is there a safety problem with a tiny scratch?"

"No, but we'll know it's there," he replied steadfastly.

I touched-up the bottom scratch, but I won't repaint the entire red sides of the hull just because the paint feels rough.

"You obviously don't understand my American work ethic," I state with frustration. "When the customer says it's good enough, it's good enough."

I win the battle (this time), although John often comes along behind me and does my work over again, his way. But I know he won't repaint the entire hull, so it's a minor victory.

* * * * *

On a mostly cloudy and cool June day, John works on the forward hatch, not satisfied with the design of the original hinges. Meanwhile, I apply the second coat of maroon to the inside of the cabin. It's a color that looked a lot better on the store's paint chart than it does on the fiberglass, and the roughness of the hull shows through. To me, it's "good enough," although I admit it looks more like purple than maroon. Inside the cabin, I want a dark lower wall (maroon) and light gray on the upper sections. John prefers white, all around.

"Looks like puke," he comments.

"Yes, but it's a bright puke. I want a vibrant interior, and this will be nice. Besides, it'll look darker when it dries."

"It'll need more coats to cover those uneven patches of fiberglass."

"This is the last coat, regardless. After all, it's a boat, and boats look good with a rough appearance."

"But it's your office," replies John.

"It's still a boat." That's my last word on the subject, or so I hope.

While I'm on my hands and knees finishing the paint job on the interior, John continues working on the forward hatch. Meanwhile, Bro barks at nothing. This dog is a terror at the airport. There are certain places that especially excite him, and this is one of them. He even chases airplanes on occasion, and that's a real problem.

A forklift approaches the hangar bay next to us from the nearby helicopter ramp. It carries a two-metre-high silver fertilizer tank on a pallet, used for aerial forestry. Bro doesn't like forklifts. Machinery, in general, is a source of irritation for this dog, and that leads to vigorous bouts of barking aimed at the metal monsters.

Bro barks up a storm, while John yells at him. The forklift driver hastens his off-load of the tank. Finally, Bro returns to the front of the hangar and lies down, awaiting the next machine (or airplane) to chase.

A few minutes later, John departs for the hardware store to buy new latches for the hatch, and I continue working inside the boat. While he is gone, I finish the second coat of maroon (not purple puke!) and prepare for my next job, the first coat of white exterior paint. Earlier this morning I purchased a gallon of expensive marine paint for this project. Now I'll need to stir it and pour it into a plastic container in preparation for painting. That is best done outside the boat.

As I prepare to exit *Gemini*, I collect what I'll need for the job. With the boat up on blocks, my descent to the hangar's dirt floor is normally accomplished with a ladder, which is usually propped against the hull. Today I decided to forgo the ladder, entering *Gemini* by climbing on the blocks, a technique that works fine when your hands aren't full. Our paint supply, including the new can of marine-white, is stored on the aft deck, so I'll need to bring it down with me, including a paint tray, roller, brush, and rags. It will be a lot quicker if I can make it in one trip, without having to retrieve the ladder from below.

I lower the sealed gallon of paint over the side, using its metal handle, aiming for the wooden blocks that support the stern. I dangle the can only inches above the block ledge. If I aim carefully, the can should easily survive a short drop.

My aim is pretty good, but the can lands slightly tilted. It hits on its bottom rim, bounces precariously on the block, and hovers briefly on the threshold of stability. But gravity wins, and the can falls from the ledge, dropping another metre to the hangar floor. It whacks down hard, bounces once, and comes to rest on its side. A tiny hole has sprouted at the bottom edge of the can where it hit the floor. Plop, plop; fizz, fizz! – white marine paint (the $70 per gallon kind) squirts out of the hole in a fine spray. White paint sprays across the dirt floor like a tiny fountain, with no sign of stopping soon.

Getting out of *Gemini* while it's up on-blocks is no easy task. But in a flash, I clamber over the side, drop down to the stern block, and hop to the ground, spurred on by my own self-directed cursing. With one hand, I grab the can and turn it upright, while snatching a nearby plastic bucket with my other hand. I drop the can in the bucket. That's all I can do for now. Two litres of white paint lies in a puddle on the dirt floor, evidence that is impossible to hide.

Before John returns from the hardware store, Rick stops by to see how *Gemini* is progressing.

"Oh, no!" he exclaims at first glance. "What happened?"

I've covered the white puddle with an old piece of boat carpet, but the paint oozes out in all directions.

"Just a minor accident," I reply.

"Has John seen this?" asks Rick, with a sense of urgency.

As if on-cue, John pulls into the hangar with his truck and hops out.

"Hi, Rick!" he yells.

He is barely out of his truck when he sees the white mess.

"Oh, no!" John's voice registers frustrated scolding.

That's the second "Oh, no!" in less than two minutes. Consider them duplicate exclamations from nearly twin brothers. Rick and John have a common disdain for inefficiency and waste.

"I shouldn't have left you alone," says John.

He's right, of course.

* * * * *

That afternoon, the rain moves in on gusty southeast winds. This is the kind of day John and I like for working in the hangar. To squander a sunny day on work when we could be up the lake or on our quads would be unbearable, so rainy days are our favorite time for work.

The open hangar allows a stiff breeze to flow through *Gemini*, swirling into her front hatch, rear door, and windows. Bro sits on the grass in front of the hangar, while the rain begins to pound more heavily. I yell at him to come inside, but he likes to sit in the rain and does so for hours, unless interrupted by the arrival of a Pacific Coastal twin-turboprop.

I hear the aircraft on its final approach, landing to the east, and I stop to watch it touch down. Bro is off in a flash, headed directly for the airplane, barking his fool head off. John yells at him to return, but Bro just keeps going until he is about two-thirds of the way to the runway. Then the twin turboprops pop into reverse with a loud "Whoosh!" that sends Bro running in circles, still barking up a storm. The airplane does a U-turn and begins to taxi back towards the terminal. Surely, the pilots see this large black dog barking threats into the air. I wonder how often their aircraft has been chased down the runway by a dog?

* * * * *

As five o'clock approaches, John begins to wrap up his work. He gathers his tools and begins to pack up things in his truck. For most of the afternoon, I have been painting the outside of the cabin with white marine paint (more $70 per gallon paint), being sure to first carefully prepare the surface to John's exacting specifications. I've roughed each segment of the surface with sandpaper and then wiped it clean with a rag. Preparation is the most demanding part of the process, since the paint itself goes on easily with a roller. Every inch of the way, John watches over me, making sure I don't cut any corners. My good-enough style of quick painting is thwarted by his must-be-perfect approach.

"I'm gonna finish up this section before I leave," I announce.

Maybe I can win a small battle here.

"Okay, I'll see you tomorrow," says John, as he finishes loading his truck.

As soon as John is gone, I hurry through the small section of outside wall with the white paint. Then I grab a piece of sandpaper and a broom. I pull myself up onto the roof of the cabin, and throw the lumber temporarily stored there onto the ground. I do a quick once-over of sandpaper on the roof's surface. Then I sweep off the residue with the broom and return to the aft deck for the white paint. I climb onto the top of the cabin again and begin slopping white paint on the roof, using what I jokingly refer to as my "American style."

In only a half hour I'm finished with the top (won't see it anyway), and hoist myself down to the aft deck. Then I superficially sand the aft wall and the area around the door. I apply a coat of marine-white, some of it covering John's still-moist bondo patches. It may be far from perfect, but it certainly is quick. In less than an hour of work, I've covered twice the area I completed before John left. It's a small victory in a never-ending battle.

* * * * *

From a seemingly hopeless project, the finished product is finally pulling together. A few coats of paint make it seem like the end is in sight. John installs the bilge pump, dabbles with minor modifications on the aft deck, and refurbishes the deteriorated windshield trim.

The electrical system is still in the design stage. A solar panel on the roof and batteries under a bench on the aft deck will support my needs nicely. Keeping the weight (lead-acid batteries) to the rear is a wise idea, since the engine has been completely removed. Large storage boxes (doubling as seats) are installed in the stern. These will be able to handle a lot of ballast.

The solar panel will serve double duty, supplying electricity for the float cabin when the boat is docked next to it. Disconnect *Gemini's* electrical umbilical cord, start the outboard kicker (to be installed someday), and I'll be able to launch for a slow-speed tour of the lake. If writing atmosphere means anything to an author, the environment has been dramatically upgraded in *Gemini*. Drift, write, and catnap on a futon to the sound of satellite radio – my dream studio. Maybe I'll hang a fishing pole over the side.

When I return from the States after a brief trip, most of the final details of the project are finished. The carpet has been installed, the remaining window trim has been painted, and the solar power system is operational. An AC inverter has been mounted on the aft wall of the cabin, wired to the batteries housed in a stern compartment. An electrical ground rod drops down below the water line mark on the transom.

Gemini's solar panel is huge, nearly twice the surface area of the float cabin's own solar panel. As it sits now, the panel almost touches the hangar roof. John assures me he will be able to rotate it flat to allow *Gemini* to be pulled out of the hangar. The electrical system will provide plenty of electrons for essentials: laptop computer, bilge pump, lights, radio, and even a ventilation fan for hot summer days.

We spend an afternoon cleaning up and making a run to the dump. The big red and white boat is finally ready, proudly sitting on its blocks in the hangar, thirteen months after I first fell in love with her classic lines. Furniture for the writer's retreat will have to be undersized or assembled inside the boat because of the small cabin door. A regular sofa can't go in, but a futon will fit, if it is laid flat. Bookcases and storage shelves can be assembled inside.

Gemini is ready to come off its blocks. From the hangar, the boat will be hauled to the launch ramp at Powell Lake. Then it will be towed to Hole in the Wall, where ballast will be added below decks for balance. We expect the boat to be bow-heavy with the engine gone, although a lot of stuff has been removed from the forward areas too. Until the hull is in the water, we won't know exactly how it will float.

Thus, this chapter comes to an end. But the project is not yet complete. It will take an additional chapter to outline the details of the unexpected. It's a tale that has a different ending than either John or I anticipate.

◊ ◊ ◊ ◊ ◊ ◊ ◊

Chapter 11

Return to Mitlenatch

After visiting Mitlenatch Island in late summer and again in winter, there is an obvious void. Walking the island in September, when the birds and summer flowers are diminishing, I am determined to return in spring when nature renews the island. April should be the perfect month to witness the return of the island's bird colonies and the explosion of wildflowers.

But April is consumed by obligations in California. Delay after delay results in a mid-May return to Powell River. A visit to Mitlenatch is a high priority, but now it might be too late to witness the island's blossoming of new life. When I arrive back in Canada in May, coastal British Columbia is basking in unusual warmth, with temperatures near 30. This premature summer will not likely fool the birds and plants of Mitlenatch. Maybe we can still capture spring on the island.

Margy and I arrive in Powell River late in the day, swooping down to Runway Zero-Nine (Runway Niner to you Americans) in our Piper Arrow. With a five-knot west wind, I still prefer landing to the east and uphill, so I forsake the light wind for the slope. Plus it brings me downward on a base leg that passes abeam John's house and a chance to waggle the wings: "Hello – we're back!"

I'm exhausted from a day of flying and the typical anxieties associated with border crossing, but the chuck at sunset is flat and inviting. Boats linger just outside the harbour, determined to squeeze the last few minutes out of a glorious day. Tomorrow's forecast calls for one more day of this false-summer warm spell. I want to use it wisely.

* * * * *

The next morning, Margy and I cruise north in the Bayliner. The 11 am temperature is already in the mid-20s, but high cirrus clouds are moving in from the west, a sign that the end is near. The distant, approaching storm provides another precursor – jet vapor trails crisscross in the high altitude air that is already gaining moisture.

The Strait of Georgia is not yet crowded, as it will be in summer, with lines of recreational vessels streaming northward. But, for now, the strait is quiet. The chuck is not as flat as it was the previous evening, but we enjoy a ride that is free of the normal ocean swells.

As we round Hurtado Point, the Lund fuel dock comes into view. It is empty of boats, with only the fuel attendant providing any sign of life, as he stands washing down the dock with a hose. This is a far cry from the crowded days of summer when it is not unusual to hover off the dock awaiting a parking spot to refuel.

As I pull in, I am a bit overconfident, regardless of my lack of experience in this boat. I aim at my desired docking spot at a 45-degree angle, but delay my final turn a moment too long, and my throttle is a bit stronger than necessary. It won't be a major crash, but it isn't going to be pretty. The fuel attendant, a teenage lad, watches my approach and sprays his hose towards me. From the command bridge I fake a ducking motion to the side, which brings a smile to the boy's face. As I finally shift into reverse, the boy cringes and drops his hose. He deftly grabs the port rail to prevent the Bayliner from crunching into the dock.

"I've forgotten how to drive!" I yell. "It's been a long winter."

He laughs and pulls the awkwardly-angled boat up against the dock, then unwraps my lines and ties them to the wooden rail.

"Gas or diesel?" he asks.

I always like that question, since bigger boats are diesels. It makes me think my boat looks bigger than it is.

"Gas," I reply.

He hands me the hose, and I begin pumping. Filling the nearly empty main and auxiliary tanks, coupled with the pump's slow flow rate, takes almost ten minutes.

After pumping for a few minutes, I tell the boy: "Let me know when I hit five dollars."

At first the young fuel attendant gives me an inquisitive grimace, but then he understands and laughs.

"That's what I remember saying when I'd pump gas into my car thirty years ago," I remark. "If you stop at five dollars these days, you'd pump less than five litres."

"It's killing boaters," he replies. "Gas prices might make this a quiet summer."

"I doubt it," I suggest. "Those damn Americans will just keep coming. With my BC flag and Canadian K-number for registration, he doesn't know I'm an American; or maybe he does.

* * * * *

Leaving Lund, I point the bow between Savary and Hernando Island. I'm without my GPS today, a loss that makes me feel uncomfortable. On the trip north in the airplane, my trusty dual-purpose GPS (with both aviation and marine data bases) simply died. Today, I revert to the original form of navigation – paper charts and eyes on the landmarks. I don't need a chart to find Mitlenatch, but the rocks off the south end of Hernando Island are of concern. Low tide is approaching, and Hernando's line of rocks extends outward several kilometres.

In reality, paper charts are nearly worthless in this situation. If you don't know these rocks, it's difficult to estimate distance from the shore. Rocks at the end of the spit are barely submerged. It's the ones you don't see that can do the damage. With a GPS receiver, you can see the otherwise invisible on that glorious invention – the moving map.

My initial course seems far enough from the tip of Hernando to escape the rocks. But as I get closer to the island, I see even more rocks extending out an amazing distance from shore during this low tide. I turn the bow further left towards Savary Island.

"Could that be Mitlenatch?" I ask Margy, as an islet appears just off the tip of Hernando. I'm surprised to see Mitlenatch Island so soon, but it has the distinctive shape – rounded on the left and double-humped.

"It's just a big rock," she replies. "They go out a long way today."

"Yes, but it has the shape of Mitlenatch, doesn't it?" I persist.

I'm now convinced she's right. It isn't Mitlenatch, and it does seem to join itself to Hernando, sitting right in the midst of the line of rocks extending out from the spit. But it sure looks like Mitlenatch.

As more rocks pop into view, we deviate even farther to the left. Suddenly, as we begin to swing past the spit, the rock that is shaped like Mitlenatch detaches itself from the rest and stands alone.

"It is Mitlenatch!" says Margy. "It sure looked like just another rock."

"And I swear it's getting smaller now, don't you think?" I reply. "So near, yet so far. The closer you get, the farther it seems."

"Unbelievable," says Margy.

The mirage-like illusion of Mitlenatch strikes again. Here's proof once more – it's an island that floats on the Strait of Georgia.

* * * * *

We arrive at Mitlenatch and begin an anti-clockwise circle of the island, surveying the shoreline while observing the 300-metres-from-shore marine park limit. Gulls sweep along the cliffs, but the large sea lion colony of winter is gone. In contrast to the dull brown of February, the island has taken on a dark green appearance.

I lower the anchor in the bay on the north side that we visited the previous September. The hook grabs snuggly. Calm seas will require little extra rope for the anchor today.

We row to shore in *Mr. Bathtub*. As Margy and I approach the gravel beach in the dinghy, gulls fly along the nearby cliffs. Many others sit on the rocky ledges or are huddled together on the beach. I hear the nearby shore-sitters squawking their calls of contentment.

We beach the dinghy and pull it up about ten metres to the high tide mark. With the tide still ebbing for two more hours, there is no need to tie it, but I knot the bow line around a nearby log anyway.

I survey the cliffs. Gulls are everywhere. Most sit about a metre from their nearest neighbor, giving each other some space, while some are nestled next to each other. The noise of the birds is loud, their high-pitched calls signaling friendship to their mates. Mixed with these calls are occasional trumpeting squawks indicating territorial claims.

The island's trails are a bit overgrown but easily navigable. We pause in the meadow near the *Marine Park* sign to inspect the wildflowers. There is a concentration of spring flowers in this area, dominated by bluish-purple Common Camas and yellow Western Buttercup. The variety of flowers is extensive throughout the island: Yellow Monkey Flower, Blue-eyed Mary, and Meadow-Death Camas (highly poisonous).

Dense thorny bushes line the trail, and a brief excursion off the path results in prickly vines cutting into my pants. Cacti thrive here too, identifying this island as a rare desert-like climate in the rain shadow of Vancouver Island.

* * * * *

We climb the path to the gull blind. The trail narrows as we near the wooden shelter, head-high brambles flanking the sides. Even as we approach the gull-covered cliff, none of the birds decide to leave. In fact, they seem oblivious to our presence. Inside the bird blind, I settle in to observe.

Directly in front of the blind's observation slats are two Glaucos-winged Gulls. They sit so close to each other that they nearly touch. Their golden-brown eyes and red bill markings are distinct identifiers of their species. The two birds emit almost soundless cak-cak calls, in contrast to the background scream of the other gulls. These birds are larger than I expected – bigger than the gulls I have seen elsewhere along the coast.

Behind the huddled pair are hundreds of smaller, white gulls with sleek lines. They are spaced like those on the cliff near the beach – about a metre apart, sometimes resting close together in pairs. Along the top of the cliff that drops off in front of us, gulls intermix with black Pelagic Cormorants, whose long craning necks point skyward. At any given moment, a few gulls are in flight in front of us, silhouetted against mountain-capped Desolation Sound to the northeast.

The noise is deafening. The gulls' abundant shrill calls are interspersed with the trumpeting squawks of: "This is my space!" To say that these birds own this island is to the say the very least.

Mixed with the calls of the birds is the sudden barking of a sea lion in the nearby east-side bay. The bark is distinctive of the California sea lion rather than the Stellers that were observed during my winter visit. When I step out of the bird blind and look towards the bay below, I count three sea lions on the distant rocks. I wonder why these have not already traveled south in their annual migration? Maybe not all of this species make the long trek to California. I ponder this mystery, but come up with no obvious answer.

I linger at the bird blind long enough to realize how lucky I am to be here on this false-summer day. I have not missed spring on Mitlenatch, after all. On a floating island, owned today by its birds and flowers, I am privileged to observe nature at its best.

Chapter 12

Upper Garden

Farming in coastal British Columbia has experienced a difficult history. The marine environment brings little snow, except to the nearby mountains, and the summer days are long and warm. Coupled with plenty of moisture, how could farming not prosper? In an area where boats are an essential part of the transportation system, getting products to market is part of the problem.

The farm at Olsen's Lake (officially Olsen Lake) is a local example of an agricultural community that once prospered, then went into decline decades ago. Similarly, Fiddlehead Farm on Powell Lake turned into a wilderness resort in an attempt to find renewed life. Fiddlehead's buildings eventually disappeared when the resort was sold for its timber. We have returned to places like this on our quads to witness the agonizing death of once-prosperous farms as they deteriorate into boggy meadows and logging slashes.

In Theodosia Valley, an older enterprise (Rupert's Farm, later called Palmer Ranch) has suffered a more gradual decay. Farm equipment and buildings have been left behind as evidence of a once booming family agricultural operation. We visit the remains and sit on an abandoned tractor, a remnant of prior decades that were much different from the Theodosia Valley of today. Twenty years ago, 60 acres of level fields around us were home to 100 head of cattle.

Dago Farm, just west of Fiddlehead, is not as well known and almost totally reclaimed by the rugged environment. John brings me here along a trail that is so overgrown I would wander off it without his guidance. As John leads me in towards a huge meadow, he points to heaps of rusting machinery lying on each side of the trail. The equipment is so deteriorated that I find it difficult to identify any of these items as being particular pieces of farm machinery.

Low scrub grows here and there, along with a few old apple trees near the far edge of the meadow, but forests have not reclaimed the fields. Dago Farm ceased operation several decades ago, but trees have not yet gained a foothold.

"It's the beavers," says John. "They built dams along the creek that flows through the meadow. Everything's flooded, and the trees can't take back the land."

From the old farm's boundary, still identified by dilapidated fences, this looks like a naturally lush, green meadow. Little brooks meander far and wide. Just getting to the outer reaches of the meadow is a task that involves circumventing several small tributaries. When we try to walk in a straight line, we have to divert in another direction while we hop across these small streams. We get back on track by leapfrogging across grassy hummocks. Larger creeks, too deep to cross, traverse the swampy meadow. One creek contains the remnants of an old beaver dam, now broken wide open, with water rushing through.

From an elevated position on a small hill at the edge of the meadow, John spies a piece of rusting machinery. I see nothing from this distance, but as we navigate closer, I finally see a dark object sticking out of a metre-high scrub bush.

By now, my hiking boots are saturated, and my socks are soaked. When we finally zigzag our way to the spot, it's a discovery worth the effort. An old harrow, once towed behind a tractor in tiller-like fashion, sits stranded in the meadow. Though totally rusted, it's still in one piece. Suspended between its two huge open-spoke steel wheels is a metal seat with a rusty vertical lever next to it. I sit on the machine, put my feet on the braces in front of the wheels, and try to move the lever. It doesn't budge.

John steps back a few feet, splashes around in the mud, and focuses his camcorder. I make vroom-vroom noises and pretend to ride the decaying metal beast. I look down at its hefty cross-frame and wipe away some of the rust with my glove. *Toronto* is imprinted in raised metal letters. It's seems that this once-valuable piece of equipment sits expectantly, awaiting renovation. If only there was a tractor to pull it and a field to plow.

"There's more here – I just know it," says John. He looks around, scouting for patches of rusty brown.

"It's kind of spooky, isn't it?"

"More sad than spooky," quips John. "Guess we'd better go."

We slip away, zigzagging our way back to our quads. It's like leaving an old cemetery where the names and faces of the dead are unknown. Many years ago, an intense battle between man and wilderness was fought here. And wilderness finally won.

* * * * *

One of Margy's construction projects at our floating cabin involves an upper garden. This small plot of reclaimed soil sits on the cliff, near the trail to our neighbor's cabin. Over the past few years, she has built this hillside spot up into a flat surface of two metres on each side. Now its vegetables supplement what comes from our floating garden. On this same spot along the cliff trail, we compost scraps from our floating garden and kitchen. In March, Margy adds a healthy amount of manure and peat to build up the plot. Then she plants potatoes.

Raids by local critters are expected. A low fence is constructed to keep the animals out, but it is a needless concern. Although I find footprints of small animals as well as larger ones (deer?), they are apparently not interested in potatoes.

The only way to get water to this site is to lug it uphill in buckets; neither efficient nor easy. Margy envisions a gravity-fed watering system, and describes it to John. In her mind's eye, water flows downhill from a hose attached to a barrel that sits on the high-ground above the garden plot.

Even with such a water system, we will need to haul water up the hill in buckets, but we can store it in the barrel. On each trip to the outhouse, we'll include a bucket of water, to be dumped into the barrel in preparation for the dry weeks of summer. When it rains, the barrel can also serve as a way to accumulate water, so I recommend adding a funnel-like collector. John is concerned with mosquitoes, so he suggests an enclosed top. The barrel will also need a way to receive our buckets of water without removing the lid each trip up the hill.

While we are in California, John begins the project, incorporating all of our suggestions. Any system John designs needs time. It must first gel in his head. This unique engineering process leads to the design excellence and product perfection I've come to expect.

When we return to Hole in the Wall in May, Margy and I climb the hill to check on the project. Along the way, we stop halfway up the cliff to inspect the spring vegetation. I look closely at an area where stonecrop flowers sprouted the previous year. These beautiful yellow flowers are a stunning sight during the early days of summer. Reddish-brown buds of this desert-like succulent plant are now intermixed with dull yellow shoots that are close to flowering. Stonecrop's yellow blanket should be abundant this year.

As we continue the climb to the upper garden, I outpace Margy and arrive first. At the split in the trail, the new watering system is not where I expect it to be. But when I glance farther uphill, I am amazed at what I see.

"Wow! Wait 'til you see this!" I yell back to Margy.

Well above the upper garden, in a location that provides optimum gravity-assist, sits a blue 55-gallon drum. Extending above it, spread out and anchored by ropes to nearby trees, is a large gray tarp. A two-by-four runs the length of the heavy-duty gray sheet, maintaining the tarp's rigidity and forcing the runoff into the barrel. A big black funnel is centered in the barrel's open plug, standing ready to collect both the runoff from rain and our buckets full of water. The barrel is braced sturdily on a flat rock base. A spigot and valve assembly at the bottom of the barrel attaches to a hose that slinks downhill to the upper garden.

Margy rounds the corner and looks up at the blue barrel, the tarp, and me.

"Oh, my! That's one massive rain collection system."

"John-built," I reply.

* * * * *

In late May, showers mix with occasional sunshine, and mid-day high temperatures hover near 20. Weak low-pressure systems alternate with fair-weather highs to produce off-and-on-again rain.

In the mornings, I wake up to find temperatures in the low teens, cold enough to justify starting a fire. It's a particularly pleasant time of the year; the air hovers between warm and cool, but almost never hot nor cold.

Today John and Bro arrive at Cabin Number 3 near noon. We launch the tin boat for Chippewa Bay, where John and his friends have recently rejuvenated a new trail down to the beach. The trail links onto an old logging road that's perfect for hiking.

It's a full boat, but soon we're cruising along on-plane. John, Margy, Bro, and me huddle on the two aft seats. John drives, as we weave along the shoreline, checking out the cabins and rocky cliffs along the way. Even though it is Victoria Day weekend, nearly all of the cabins are empty; most locals are waiting for warmer, sunnier days to move into their summer homes on the lake. Our cabin, occupied in all seasons, is the exception rather than the rule.

We all enjoy the ride, but no one is happier about it than Bro. Tin boats are his favorite. As John's constant companion, Bro spends a lot of time in boats, but he's usually a nervous passenger. He often shakes and shivers for the entire ride. Tin boats are the exception. He loves the wide-open feel of small vessels, poking his nose over the side like a dog sticking his head out of the car window. Bro sits calmly and without a shiver or shake today, even occasionally lying down in the bottom of the hull, contentedly curled up.

John points the boat towards shore at the far end of Chippewa Bay. It's a gravelly shore, with pockets of small rocks mixed with huge granite boulders. This is the starting point for today's hike (and termination of the new trail). We haul the boat up onto the beach and tie the bow line to a small tree.

John's attention is on a skookum log that has drifted onto the beach, half-floating against the shore. I help him break the log loose, using thick branches as pry-bars, until the six-metre-long log floats freely. John hammers a staple into the end and uses a rope from the boat to tie the log to a stump on the beach. Upon our return from today's hike, we'll tow it back to Hole in the Wall, perfect as a breakwater reinforcement.

From our landing spot on the beach, the trail is completely hidden. But in just a few steps up from the shoreline, we are on the nicely groomed path. Bro leads, sniffing the ground and inspecting the trail from side to side. The path leads to an old logging road, where we turn left and then shortly exit onto a well-worn trail that winds uphill.

Bro sniffs intently for bears. He pauses occasionally to examine the fresh scat that is scattered along the trail. I remove my trusty knife and put it in my pocket where it will be readily available. It's a habit that makes little sense as defense against a bear, but it makes me feel better.

"I have my knife ready for bears, just in case," I boast, expecting John to laugh at my knife.

"Might see a bear today," says John, with a glance at my knife that tells me he's not impressed. "They've been out of hibernation a few weeks, and this is a prime spot to find a momma and her cub. It never hurts to be prepared."

Trees only three metres high flank the old logging road, part of the replanting process after logging stripped the area. This is the season for lush undergrowth and new blossoms; tips of branches stand out in light green buds, heralding spring's renewal.

Bro continues to sniff and scout for bears, and we keep a watch for anything he might stir up from the nearby bush. At a turnoff, John leads us down a trail to a pond, where Bro goes frog hunting behind a beaver dam, while we rest and talk about trees.

"What's that one?" asks John, pointing to a one-metre-high seedling growing in the middle of the trail near the beaver dam.

"Cedar," I reply confidently. The flat, wide-spread needles are a dead give-away, but I find it tougher to identify big cedars when the branches are higher from the ground with only the trunk's bark patterns to provide clues.

"Not bad," he says. "Look at those three firs right next to each other. One is green and alive, the one next to it has even more buds busting out all over the place, and the third one is dead."

Seeing these small trees side-by-side is perplexing. They are obviously of the same age, about ten years old. One is dark green and healthy looking, with no buds at all, while the next one displays lots of light green new growth. And the third is covered with dead, dark-red needles. Why would these three trees develop so differently? There is no obvious answer — maybe it's like brothers who are genetically related but can be so different in individual characteristics, including their health.

"How about that one?" asks John, motioning to a tree standing by itself with protruding finger-length buds.

"Scotch Pine," I state, confident it is a pine because of its skinny needles.

"Close enough," says John. "We call them Jack Pines."

John spots an eagle soaring high up against the mountainside, and points it out to us. Margy and I scan the area and finally see the bird that John spotted so easily.

A woodpecker rat-a-tat-tats in the background, and John gives us another lesson in paying close attention to nature.

"That's a woodpecker, of course. But do you hear that fainter sound of a grouse over by the road?"

I hear the sound, a dull thumping noise, but it sounds like "Thumper," a mysterious noise I described in *Up the Main* (Chapter 9) as the rubbing of trees in the wind. Could I have mistakenly lied to my readers and myself?

"That's a grouse?" asks Margy, looking at me with an inquisitive eye. I know what she is saying. We arrived in Powell River only two days ago from the States, and heard a similar sound in Hole in the Wall. We both agreed that Thumper was back, indicating pecker poles up on the hillside were rubbing against each other in the breeze. Margy's glance now suggests I have been caught abusing my author's poetic license.

But the resonant thump of this grouse flapping its wings is slightly different from the sound I call "Thumper," so maybe both John and I are right. This is a grouse, and the noise in the Hole is the sound of trees rubbing against each other; rationalization at its best.

We leave the beaver pond, join the main road, and continue farther up the trail. Along the road, hemlocks and dogwoods add to the mix of trees.

The next major dip in the road is followed by a substantial uphill stretch, so I suggest we reverse course. I'm wimpy but wise, since we have a considerable hike back to the boat.

During our return to the beach, Bro doesn't give up his hunt for even a moment. But we don't see any bears.

The water in Chippewa Bay is amazingly warm compared to the rest of the lake. It will be mid-June before we dare jump into the deep swimming hole behind Cabin Number 3, but already in May this shallow beach is warm enough for a dip. We all take off our shoes and socks; except Bro, who is already in the water and swimming in wide circles. I strip down and go in up to my chest. Margy stays dressed in her T-shirt and shorts, and braves the water up to her hips. John (a warm-water only swimmer) rolls up his pant legs and sloshes in up to his knees. John and I pull small rocks from the shallow water and toss them back and forth, trying to catch them but seldom succeeding before they splash beside us. Pretty soon we have all have had enough of the not-too-warm water (except Bro) and are ready to leave.

John prepares the log we have set aside for towing, attaching it to the tin boat's transom rope. As soon as we get underway, the log's mass takes command, pulling us off course to the side. Then it settles down behind the boat, trailing us without much trouble. John is able to increase speed a few knots, and we settle into a slow but comfortable cruise back to Hole in the Wall.

Since we will not be riding on-plane, Margy moves to the front of the boat, and I stretch out in the seat near the middle. John drives, and Bro scrunches down in front of him for a nap.

I'm seldom sleepy in a boat, but today is an exception. The warm May sun beats down, and the water is smooth. The tin boat drones along slowly, with the log in-tow.

I stretch out sideways on the metal seat, propping my head against my backpack, hanging my feet over the side, shutting my eyes, and enjoying the ride. A few minutes later, I force my sleepy eyes open and catch a glimpse of a nearby granite cliff plummeting into the water. I cat-nap contentedly as we slowly slip out of Chippewa Bay along its steep-sided mountains.

* * * * *

The next morning, Victoria Day (Monday), it is raining again. I think about Canadian families who have ventured out on their first camping trip of the almost-here summer season. This is a popular time for camping, and I am sorry that their long weekend will end with rain. But then I selfishly consider other impacts of this precipitation.

From the front deck of the cabin, I yell to Margy: "We're making water!"

I visualize the rain dripping down through the forest canopy near the upper garden, running along the collecting tarp, and dripping into the storage barrel. Rain can be miserable; it can be consoling; and it can be precious when it's filling your rain barrel.

I'm proud that I'm not completely dependent on man-made sources of energy. When the sun shines (especially in the winter), I often declare: "We're making electricity!" Our solar panel produces power during the day, but it is not enough on short, often-cloudy winter days. So, when the wind blows (especially at night) and our wind generator whirls, I yell: "We're making electricity!"

Now we have a new addition to this celebration of natural resources. When it rains, I can proclaim: "We're making water!" Well, we may not be making water, but we are collecting it for the upper garden.

I climb the steps to the outhouse, and continue on up to the trail junction. Then I turn towards the path leading to the tarp strung between the trees. The rainfall here, under the thick branches, is hardly noticeable. But the tarp is spotted with big beads of water, and narrow rivulets flow towards the funnel. Water is collecting along the two-by-four at the center of the tarp, and large drops drip off each side of the board into the funnel. The drops fall nearly in unison from each side of the board. It's a steady *drip, drip, drip.*

I tap the barrel to try to determine how full it is. The water is over two-thirds to the top, considerably fuller since my last check the previous day. With small drops, large barrels will be filled. It takes a while, but I have lots of time; and rain in coastal BC can be depended upon.

* * * * *

That evening, after a day of off-and-on rain, I climb the hill to use the outhouse, and I carry a bucket of water for the rain barrel. It is getting dark, but not so dark that I can't see the rain barrel and its tarp in the small clearing. I step up to the large funnel and begin to pour from my bucket. The water immediately fills the funnel and begins to overflow onto the ground. The barrel is already full.

We're making water.

◊ ◊ ◊ ◊ ◊ ◊

Chapter 13

The Bottom of Powell Lake

Now that I have some microscope experience, I turn my thoughts to the bottom of Powell Lake. I still have no definite plan, but the possibility of retrieving a deep-water sample for inspection under my microscope is too appealing to ignore.

Margy finds a bright orange electrical cord-reel at the thrift store for two dollars. Although we haven't yet decided whether rope or heavy fishing line will be used, this plastic reel is the second part for the master plan (the first being my microscope). One evening, when John isn't home, I leave the reel in his garage as an enticement. I include a note supposedly signed by *Jacques Cousteau* that dubs this new challenge: "Deep Water Retrieval Project." When John's dad, Ed, hears my name for the project, he nixes it: "What we need is a scientific title with an appropriate acronym," Ed says. "Something that'll get some attention."

I immediately accept his challenge, thinking through a variety of phrases that will produce an appropriate series of initials. If a pipe is used for the collecting of water specimens, the project can be called DRIP (Deep Recovery in Pipe). Better yet, if we use a bottle, it could be DRIBBLE (Deep Recovery in Bottle Below Lake Elevation). I visualize my boat hovering over the deepest part of the lake, with a large, ominous sign mounted on the stern: *Stay Clear! – DRIBBLE in-progress.*

At first, John favors using rope (1000 feet is a lot of rope) with manual deployment and an electrical triggering mechanism. Because of the greater water pressure at the anticipated depth of 1000 feet, John recommends that we use a metal pipe for the collection mechanism.

I remind him this is a project on a budget, and the budget doesn't involve the deep pockets of the Canadian government.

I consult "The Doc," a friend and geologist who specializes in oceanography. He refers me to an Internet site where expensive Niskin bottles can be purchased. My suspicions are confirmed – marine scientists do sample deep water routinely, but at great expense.

Another friend from my pseudoscience past is Frank, less of a scientist and more of a nature lover. He works as an instructor in an oceanography lab at a community college near San Francisco. When he accompanies his students on the college's research vessel in the San Francisco Bay, he operates a device called a Kemmerer bottle to obtain water samples at depths much less than the bottom of Powell Lake. Frank has access to research-quality water collection bottles and seems willing to bring one to Canada in return for a quad riding adventure in the wilderness. I appreciate the offer, but this raises more problems than it solves. The Kemmerer bottle doesn't have enough rope to lower it 1000 feet into the lake. Two long ropes will be needed – one for the bottle and another for the "messenger weight" which is used to trip the valves closed. This seems too complicated for my proposed drop into Powell Lake.

Frank's prognosis for the project is not encouraging: "What do you expect to discover down there?" he asks. "Don't count on finding anything alive at that depth."

Though I don't expect to find microbial life at 1000 feet, I hate to give up on this project. I have come a long way in my attempts to find an appropriate and affordable deep-drop apparatus. The challenge of obtaining a water sample from the bottom of Powell Lake remains enticing.

* * * * *

Frank and I aren't able to come up with a specific plan for the Kemmerer bottle that works for us both. But just when I decide the DRIP (or DRIBBLE) project is now far in the future, Frank contacts me with an unexpected surprise. He has located a Kemmerer bottle that he can loan to me for an indefinite period. He isn't able to make it to Powell River this summer, but he can give me a bottle on my next trip from Los Angeles to Canada, if I can arrange to pick it up in San

Francisco. I can keep it until the drop is complete or his college finds out it is missing; whichever comes first.

In mid-May, I depart Los Angeles for Powell River in my Arrow. The first stop is Concord, near San Francisco, where Frank awaits with the Kemmerer bottle and a lesson regarding how to deploy the apparatus.

In the lobby at Concord Airport, Frank explains how the end valves of the container (called a "bottle," although its made of metal) are opened and locked into position for the drop. He uses a short length of rope to demonstrate how the five-pound lead weight (which he simulates by pointing to the end of the line) should be attached a few feet below the bottle. Then he shows me how the messenger weight is dropped down the rope. *Clank!* – the cylindrical messenger strikes the top of the bottle and the valves snap shut, trapping the water sample inside.

"There's no second line for the messenger?" I ask. I expected two lines in this design, but I see only one.

"It all fits on one rope," replies Frank. "That's what makes this setup so efficient. Of course, you're going to need 1000 feet of rope."

"How about fishing line? – the heavy stuff, at least 60-pound test," I suggest. "Maybe I could deploy it using a fishing rod, and that would take care of how to spool the extra line."

"I think you should use rope," says Frank in an uncharacteristically stern tone.

I can see the concern in his face. If this Kemmerer bottle doesn't return from the bottom of the lake, he's in trouble.

"Okay, I'll find a long rope. I already have an old cord reel that may be able to handle a thousand feet of line."

We say our goodbyes, and Frank hurries off to an appointment at his college, leaving me in the airport lobby with the two-foot long metal bottle. I'm fiddling with the messenger weight when Frank reappears at the side door of the lobby. His car is double-parked outside as he yells through the door.

"Hey, I came back to tell you I just thought of a way you can cover the rental charges for the bottle," he offers. "Bring me back a sample for my class to analyze in the lab."

"That's an easy price to pay. I'll call you on my satellite phone from the middle of the lake, if I need help."

Franks laughs, wishes me "Good luck!" and hurries on his way.

A few minutes later, back at my airplane, I realize I forgot to give Frank the gift I am carrying for him in my backpack. It's a book about the first atomic bomb, a subject that interests both of us. When I read the book, I thought of Frank, and set it aside for him. Now I've missed the chance to show my appreciation for the loan of the Kemmerer bottle. Maybe it's not too late.

Frank won't be able to return to the airport now, since he's already late for his appointment, but I can leave the book at the counter in the airport lobby. I phone Frank and leave a message on his voicemail explaining that he should return to the airport later to pick up a gift at the airport lobby.

Back at the Arrow, I find a paper bag and wrap it around *The Bomb* (by Gerard DeGroot), tying it with a few feet of dental floss I find in my backpack. Then I write Frank's name on the bag and take it to the lobby. I ask the woman behind the counter to hold the package for Frank's pickup. She looks at the floss-tied bundle with mistrust, stares at me with keen eyes, and then nods her reluctant acceptance of the package. After I walk away, I realize that an airport lobby is not the best place to leave a book about atomic bombs.

* * * * *

When I arrive back in Powell River, I visit Jim's marine shop to purchase some test rope for an initial shallow-water drop in Powell Lake. I decide that 3/16-inch rope will work best. I explain to Jim how I plan to collect water from the bottom of the lake. He nods his head, but his eyebrows are raised in skepticism. I tell Jim I'll give his shop credit for the rope if I make it big in *Maclean's* magazine. He simply nods his head again and measures off the rope from the spool. I leave the shop with 100 feet of rope and a five-pound lead weight.

* * * * *

At my cabin the next day, I thread the rope through the Kemmerer bottle, lock open the valves, and attach the five-pound weight. Then I hold the bottle as high as I can reach. I clip the messenger to the line and drop it. It clanks against the bottle, and the valves slam shut, exactly as advertised.

I step aboard the Campion to get a clear area for my first test drop. Here, off the boat's side, I will not entangle the bottle's rope with the cabin's floating structure.

I lower the weight and bottle into the water and let the rope slip through my hands. The weight takes the bottle down quickly. The rope runs fast enough through my fingers to cause an immediate and painful rope burn.

"Yikes!" I yell, as I let go of the rope.

Margy, who is standing nearby on the cabin's deck, is horrified.

"You let go of the rope?" she yells.

"Rope burn! The bottle will hit bottom before the line runs out."

I hope.

"Oh, good. I thought you'd lost the bottle. Frank would kill you."

True, but what about my poor hand?

The test is still under control. I'm surprised that the buoyancy of the water does little to slow the descent of the bottle and the five-pound weight. The bottle disappears quickly into the depths. It may be nearly 100 feet deep here, so I'll need to be ready to stop the bottle's descent before running out of rope. Get ready for another rope burn! How about gloves next time?

But the rope stops unwinding with plenty of line remaining on the deck. There's about 30 feet left, so the bottle is down 70 feet.

I grab the rope, snap the messenger weight onto it, and drop the small cylindrical weight down the line with a splash. I feel the messenger descending, my rope-hand sensing the vibration of the wobbling weight. In a few seconds, I detect a distinct *thump* as the weight whacks against the top valve of the Kemmerer bottle.

I pull the whole apparatus back to the surface, wrapping the rope around my arm from elbow to hand. It is not difficult to raise the bottle, but it does take more muscle than expected. I try to imagine the effort that will be required for manual retrieval from a depth of 1000 feet.

I haul the bottle and the dangling weight out of the water, a procedure that takes both hands once the bottle and lead weight break the surface. Then I push the spring-loaded water drain valve to dump a sample into two small plastic bottles that stand ready for the occasion. The test drop is a big success, but I'll need to solve the rope burn hazard before making the deep water drop.

* * * * *

I let the water samples from the test drop stand for a few hours. Then I place my microscope onto the picnic table. When I flip on the internal light, it is dead. Rather than recharge the lamp, I experiment with the alternate light source, using the hinged mirror; just like my days in Biology 101. I detach the light and install the mirror, angling it towards the brightly illuminated afternoon sky to the south. The binocular eyepieces provide a bright field of view.

Under low magnification, there is a lot to see in this water sample taken from 70 feet deep. I inspect microscopic bits of algae, greenish-brown and definitely plantlike. Tinier specimens drift in slow motion across the microscope's field of view. At first it looks like abundant animal life, but it is only the natural flow of the water. Tiny particles swirl slowly, in concert with the flow. What will I find in water over ten times as deep?

Using increased magnification, the objects show no internal motion or flagella, but the sample contains an interesting variety of specimens. One long, thin red thread reminds me of spirogyra from a biology textbook.

I try another sample of water, this time using one of my concave-recessed slides to hold three drops of water. There is more to see now, but it is difficult to focus on the objects in the eyepieces. The thickness of the sample is enough to cause problems; I must constantly refocus to view objects at various depths within the concave cavity. The overall results are the same – obvious plant life, evident by its greenish-brown algae-like structure. I can identify extensive cell structure, but no signs of animals in motion.

* * * * *

Dropping the Kemmerer bottle to the bottom of Powell Lake is going to succeed – I can just feel it. All that I need to do is fine tune the final details. In the meantime, I research the history of previous deep-water studies in Powell Lake.

The University of British Columbia conducted its initial research at Powell Lake in 1961. UBC's Institute of Oceanography confirmed that the lake has a bottom layer of salt water, beginning at a depth of about 400 feet below the surface, with salinity increasing with depth. At the bottom, the scientists discovered water that is half as salty as the Strait of Georgia. The samples they recovered in 1961 were deemed the oldest trapped seawater yet discovered anywhere in the world. Scientists concluded that the water at the deepest part of Powell Lake contains no oxygen and no life other than bacteria.

A more extensive UBC study, conducted in 1971, concentrated on the temperature microstructure of Powell Lake. In a series of deep drops using equipment that was sophisticated at the time, scientists studied the flat-bottomed basins in the southern portion of the lake. One of the prime research sites was located mid-channel, just north of Three-Mile Bay.

The 1971 data confirmed the earlier water profiles of the 1961 study. Lake temperature declines with depth to 300 feet (temperature 2 degrees C), and then warms again as depth increases. At 800 feet, temperatures exceed surface water temperature. Dissolved oxygen, not surprisingly, decreases with depth, with none below 400 feet. Salinity first appears at a depth of about 400 feet, increasing gradually to a depth of 800 feet, and then increasing more rapidly at the lake's deepest points. (*Journal of Physical Oceanography*, 1971, Volume 3, page 302.)

Powell Lake is one of the deepest lakes in British Columbia, with a maximum recorded depth of 1180 feet. The overall water profile of the lake shows colder fresh water flowing over warmer salt water. The scientific studies of the 1960s and 1970s whet my appetite. I want to get going with my own deep drop.

* * * * *

I consult with John and Ed, showing them Frank's Kemmerer bottle. I demonstrate how the messenger weight clicks the valves shut. I visualize the messenger weight slipping down 1000 feet of line to make contact with the bottle at the bottom of Powell Lake.

The bottle's drift during the drop is one of our biggest concerns. This can be partially solved by using a heavier lead weight; I decide to increase the weight from five to fifteen pounds. After changing my mind numerous times, I finally select the line to be used for the drop: a #15 tarred nylon seine twine normally used for fish netting. The price of the line is reasonable, and the strength seems adequate for the task. The unknown effects of drift may add considerable tension to the line, but I fully expect to return the Kemmerer bottle to Frank; or hide from him forever.

* * * * *

Using the wide aft deck of the Bayliner, I make several test drops on the chuck, using the smaller five-pound weight and the original (thicker but shorter) 3/16-inch rope. Using the five-pound weight and the test rope, I perform test drops in Squirrel Cove and Theodosia Inlet. These drops take the Kemmerer bottle into depths less than a tenth of what is expected in Powell Lake. All the tests go well, but I'm concerned about dropping the Kemmerer bottle into 1000 feet of water. What if the drift tension on the thinner line cause the Kemmerer bottle to break loose, or suppose the bottle becomes lodged on the bottom? How will I ever tell Frank?

* * * * *

On a sunny day in late October, I consolidate everything needed for the deep drop. I spend the morning on the cabin deck, unwrapping the spool of twine. I pull the seine cord from its packaged spool and mark it with tape every 100 feet. As the line drops onto the deck, Margy winds all 1500 feet of it onto the orange plastic reel. We're now prepared for a drop to a depth of over 1000 feet, with spare line to accommodate the expected drift. My goal is to drop into one of the deepest spots in Powell Lake, just north of Three-Mile Bay.

Margy and I assemble the equipment, threading the twine into the metal tube that runs through the center of the Kemmerer bottle. We add two metres of rope at the bottom of the bottle to hold the heavier 15-pound weight. Then I lock the end valves of the Kemmerer bottle open. I hoist it over the edge of the deck and prepare for a test drop into 70 feet of water. As soon as I lift the bottle and its attached weight, it's obvious that the heavier weight is going to be a problem. This time I wear work gloves, but the thin twine still digs into my fingers. In fact, I'm not sure how I'm going to be able to slowly release the bottle without cutting my fingers. So I clumsily toss the whole apparatus into the water. Margy grabs the handle on the orange cord-reel to slow the descent of the heavy weight, gradually lowering the bottle to the bottom.

Once the bottle is down, I clip the messenger weight to the cord and drop it. In a few seconds, I feel a distinct *whack*, as the messenger makes contact with the Kemmerer bottle. The plastic reel will be too flimsy to raise the bottle and its heavy weight, so I begin to heft it up to the surface using hand-over-hand pulls on the line. Even with a second pair of gloves layered over the first, the twine digs into my fingers. The bottle and lead weight will be impossible to haul up from a depth of 1000 feet.

After this brief test, it's obvious we must return to the lighter five-pound weight, regardless of any drift we may encounter during the deep drop. Margy and I repeat the test over the side of the cabin's deck using the smaller weight. I wear three layers of gloves this time. Pulling the mechanism back up to the deck is a sluggish and barely acceptable procedure. I feel my arm muscles begin to ache after making two test drops to a depth of only 70 feet. We'd better get going with the deep drop before I change my mind.

* * * * *

I position our boat mid-channel, about two kilometres north of Three-Mile Bay. We drift, engine off, in one-foot waves and moderate winds. The Bayliner is the perfect boat for the deep drop, and so is the timing. I've recently moved this boat to our cabin for a fresh-water winter lay-over on Powell Lake. The boat's aft deck provides a solid, roomy work area for the project.

Because of today's conditions, the Bayliner will be pushed to the northeast during the drop. But that should still keep us positioned over the deepest part of the lake. This is near the spot where UBC ocean-ographers successfully took deep water samples during four drops in 1971. On their fifth drop, a bit farther south, they failed to retrieve their expensive scientific equipment.

I jot down a GPS reading of latitude and longitude and hoist the Kemmerer bottle and the five-pound weight over the side. Margy uses the handle on the plastic reel to control the descent, while I allow the twine to slip through my triple-gloved hands. I'm careful not to miss the plastic 100-foot tape markers as they slide between my fingers. I begin counting the depth marks: *100 feet, 200, 300, 400.* The drop goes flawlessly.

As we pass 700 feet, I ask Margy to slow the descent rate to assure we don't miss contact with the bottom. She's sitting in the middle of the aft deck, straddling the reel and controlling the drop rate, while I let the line slip through my hand. It seems unlikely I will be able to feel the thump of the weight against the lake's floor. Thus, I'm concerned that the Kemmerer bottle may fall horizontally onto the bottom, risking contamination with the silt on the floor of the lake. Worse yet, a bottle resting horizontally on the bottom may not be able to snap closed when the messenger weight drops down the line.

It's unlikely we'll reach the lake's deepest recorded depth of 1180 feet, but I hope for at least 800 feet. Anything over 1000 feet will be cause to celebrate. According to the UBC 1971 drop report, we are now floating over the southern end of a flat-bottomed basin where the lake's deepest soundings have been recorded.

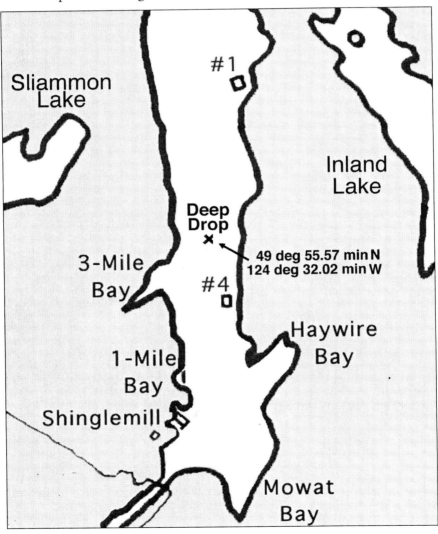

As the line passes through my gloves, I feel the flick of the 900-foot marker. I ask Margy to slow the descent even more. Occasionally she stops the reel so I can bob the line. I'm trying to determine whether the feel of the line has changed, indicating bottom contact.

We pass 1000 feet, Margy now unwinding the line only a few feet at a time. Then, just as the 1100-foot marker slides through my hand, I feel the bottom. I jig with the twine wrapped around my hand, definitely sensing the weight bob against the lake's floor. It's remarkably like jigging with an ocean lure. Even at this extreme depth, the feel of bottom is almost the same.

I carefully attach the messenger weight, and release it down the line. I feel the wobble of the spinning weight zooming down the twine, rapidly accelerating. In less than a minute, the whirling is replaced by a noticeable thump, as the messenger hits the bottle. I'm amazed how fast it reaches the bottom and that I can actually feel the weight hit the valve at a depth of 1100 feet.

I'm jubilant! Now, if only the bottle's valves have closed.

I begin to heft the whole apparatus up to the surface. My most effective retrieving motion is a repetitious hand-over-hand pull. My gloves provide adequate protection, but the 100-foot markers are slow to reappear. When my arms tire, I step over the line to use a different set of muscles at a slightly different angle. About every 50 feet of the retrieval, I step back over the twine to obtain a new position from which to pull, but my arm muscles are getting really sore.

During the half-hour it takes to retrieve the line, three workboats pass nearby, all going south. The sun is now dipping behind the Bunster Range, and loggers are headed home. Each boat's captain is probably inspecting us closely. (What is that boat doing, engine stopped in the middle of this deep channel, with fishing season over?) I'm sure the occupants of these vessels are watching to see if we are in trouble. I wave at each boat with a friendly swing of my free arm so they know we are not in distress.

Another boat, a sporty runabout, pulls even closer as it travels south.

"He's reducing power," observes Margy, as the boat slowly approaches. "I think he's going to stop."

"You okay?" asks a man who's positioned in the open aft deck of the mostly canvas-covered boat, as his boat drifts gradually past our stern.

"No problems," I reply.

Must I explain? It will be difficult. Margy sits straddling the orange reel in the middle of the aft deck, while I lean over the side, struggling to retrieve something from one of the deepest spots in the lake.

"Beautiful day," says the boater. "Just wanted to make sure you weren't in trouble."

"Thanks for stopping to check on us."

I'm grateful for his concern, but I'd prefer not to explain further. ("Oh, we're just floating around here, dropping a metal bottle over the side, down to about 1000 feet.")

Like most local boaters, this fellow is concerned with the safety of others on the lake, but he's not about to pry into our business. He waves a friendly good-bye and speeds away.

By now, both Margy and I have lost track of the twine markers. Some seem to have disappeared, maybe ripped loose by the rapidly descending messenger weight. I look over the side repeatedly, hoping for a glimpse of the Kemmerer bottle.

I pull and pull, my arms now nearly exhausted. I take a few brief rests, but I'm anxious to get the Kemmerer bottle up to the surface and to secure our prize water sample inside the awaiting plastic container.

There it is! The metal cylinder is only ten feet below me, and the top valve looks closed!

I slowly haul the bottle over the gunnel, careful not to hit it on the hull or handrails. The bottle is closed and dribbling a little from its bottom drain. Now, with only a few feet to go, I don't want to risk accidentally popping the valves open. I lower the five-pound weight onto the floor of the aft deck, keeping the bottle vertical and positioned near the plastic container. Margy grabs the Kemmerer bottle and aligns it with the neck of the one-gallon container. She bends low, depresses the spring-loaded drain valve, and immediately backs away to arms length when the smell hits her.

"Yuck! That's nasty!" Margy exclaims. "Smells like rotten eggs."

"And look how yellow it is!"

I had expected normal looking water. Instead, this looks and smells like no other liquid I have ever seen. It has an opaque brownish-yellow hue. The smell is overpowering. The 1971 UBC analysis indicates this deep lake water contains considerable methane and hydrogen sulfide, with no dissolved oxygen. It's a prehistoric mix, 10,000 years old!

* * * * *

Back at the cabin, I uncap the plastic container to pour some of the yellow, fetid water into a small jar. The smell of rotten eggs is overwhelming. I allow the water to sit in the jar (now capped), providing time for any particles to settle in preparation for my microscopic inspection. In the next few hours, a dull white opaque layer precipitates to the bottom of the jar. I will later theorize this is the result of the sulfides encountering free oxygen for the first time in 10,000 years, with the end result being the formation of hydrogen sulfate.

How could any plant or animal live in this foul goop? Then again, life is both resilient and adaptive, as has been proven in nature many times. Life thrives near volcanic vents on the ocean's floor and even in the dense inner layers of rocks in Antarctica. Why not at the bottom of Powell Lake? Samples of this odd looking (and smelling) water, sealed in small jars, will make unique gifts for friends of Powell River Books. I'm tempted to add *Do Not Drink* to the label, but not everyone appreciates my sense of humor.

I focus the microscope on a slide prepared from drops extracted from the jar. I spy the normal clutter of small contaminants. The microscopic view is similar to the near-surface samples I've studied. Complex structures are evident, and the quantity of these structures is typical of samples taken from much shallower depths.

Some of what I see under magnification looks like typical microscopic plant life, but I conclude that part of what I am viewing includes contaminates caught within the Kemmerer bottle during the sampling process; this was not a scientifically sterile experiment. Yet, some of what I see in the microscope may be local residents of the yellow water. As expected, nothing on the slide is moving. But the water sample is less barren than I had anticipated. The results are pleasing, although the focus of this project has changed over time. As the project has developed, the microscopic observations have become less important than the sampling procedure.

Many scientific explorations do not achieve their originally intended goals. Here is a fine example. Initially, this project was designed to observe a deep-water sample under a microscope. Over time, that objective became less important, eventually being replaced by the challenge of the sampling process itself. How to obtain a water sample from the depths of Powell Lake became an exciting challenge, and hauling the Kemmerer bottle aboard the boat was a joyous moment.

The greatest thrill of the project included the shock of discovering the yellow, foul-smelling water and the strange precipitate that developed after contact with air. What a substantial (and smelly) surprise! The journey to the goal – and finally getting there – has made all of the difference in the world.

◊ ◊ ◊ ◊ ◊ ◊ ◊

Chapter 14

Down the Strait

In my first years of residence in Powell River, I kayaked around some of the small islands and shorelines on the east side of southern Vancouver Island. In addition to the Cedar-by-the-Sea overnight trip documented in *Up the Lake* (Chapter 19), John and I kayaked Lady-smith Harbour near Nanaimo. Bro rode in *Mr. Kayak's* center seat, with John in the rear (controlling the rudder) and me in front. The log booms of Ladysmith were the highlight of that paddling excursion, as we watched a "dozer" work the pens. This small-but-tough caged boat used bursts of power to push logs every which way. Even the huge, over-sized prop of this work-boat is enclosed in steel mesh to protect it from deadheads. If running a crane at a loading dock were a typical man's dream, operating a dozer would be John's idea of ecstasy.

On this two-day trip, John and I launch *Mr. Kayak* at a small marina on the lower Courtney River, adjacent to the airport. This area is a favorite for local bird watchers (of both the natural and metallic breeds). You can stroll the paved path around the airport, observing the numerous birds that frequent this marshy area. At the same time, you'll pass seaplanes taking off and landing in the Courtney River and wheeled aircraft operating on the paved runway. It's a peaceful small airport location that is in stark contrast to the high security norm of bigger airports.

The marina includes an excellent boat ramp, perfect for kayaks, with plentiful nearby parking. Salt water sloshes in from the ocean, but fresh water pouring down the Courtney River, provides automatic cleansing on the hulls of boats docked here. The marshy entrance from the ocean is usable only when the tide is high. The marina is nearly land-locked at low tide, but kayaks can get through.

From this marina, we start a short but demanding paddle up the river to "The Slough" and the touristy downtown marina. Low tide, however, prevents us from crossing the sand bar at the marina's entrance. Even in our shallow-draft kayak, we must give up and get out of the kayak to turn around.

"Bro, you stay there," says John.

Bro looks up from his center seat, not about to budge from his dry cocoon, as John and I awkwardly maneuver the kayak around in the shallow entrance. Bro sits straight up in his seat like a king in an open carriage. From here, we return down the river to our launch site, riding a pleasant push from the current.

Before pulling the kayak out of the water, I want to try a solo paddle out of the lower portion of the almost-dry channel that connects to the ocean. It's a route experienced boaters won't attempt in low water like this, since the small river runs wide and shallow through this delta. Even at high tide, boaters must carefully maneuver through the middle of the narrows by following large flat-board alignment markers.

On parts of this winding route, I walk *Mr. Kayak* through ankle-deep water, eventually exiting into Comox Harbour where the water is deep. John and Bro are waiting for me with the Ford Tempo.

On this same trip to Vancouver Island, we stay overnight in a downtown Nanaimo hotel. Worried about hotel rules regarding pets, I call ahead to ask if they allow dogs.

"Sure. But there's a ten dollar fee for pets," replies the reservation clerk.

I'm relieved. John planned to sneak Bro into the room, but I feel uncomfortable with that. I'm glad to pay the fee.

"Okay, we'll reserve a room and pay the extra fee for a dog," I state.

"What size – the dog, that is?" asks the clerk.

I wasn't expecting this. Maybe they don't allow large dogs.

"Oh, I'd say he's medium size," I reply, realizing I am far understating Bro's stature.

Upon arrival in the room, Bro is greeted by a treat of milk bones and an undersized dog bed; and I do mean undersized.

"Look at that tiny bed," laughs John. "How do they expect Bro to sleep in that thing?"

I am too embarrassed to tell him about my misguided white lie.

The next morning, we return to the Tempo to find *Mr. Kayak* in distress. During the night, kayak thieves attempted to steal him from the sturdy rooftop racks. Apparently, these crooks didn't anticipate a John-designed rack. The boat bandits couldn't cut through the reinforced locked cable (kayak to rack), so they tried to pry the metal roof racks loose. Both kayak and racks survived, but the racks were bent in the failed attempt.

It was a great sense of relief to know that *Mr. Kayak* survived an attempted kidnapping. I'm grateful that John built such a hefty rooftop rack. I recall John's astonishment that this was the way things are in the big city – dog beds are puny, and kayak thieves are rampant on every corner.

* * * * *

Paddling the southern Gulf Islands remained high on my list of things to do. The many small islands in this area can be reached directly from Vancouver Island, but this involves considerable open-water paddling. It's not dangerous, but it is tiring and time consuming. A better alternative is to launch from an island that is accessible by ferry; Margy and I choose Thetis Island as our launching point.

On a mid-August morning, we take the first ferry from Powell River to Comox. After boarding, Margy snaps a photo of me in front of the Tempo with *Mr. Kayak* on top.

"You're not from here?" inquires a friendly fellow who exits his van in front of us.

Oh, great. I look like a tourist, even with my BC license plates and Powell Lake T-shirt. It must be the *Cal* hat.

"From Powell River," I proudly state.

"Oh, I thought you were a tourist. They're always taking pictures on the ferry."

To be truthful, I don't ride the ferries often, so this is a tourist-like experience for me.

"The photos are for my wife's mother in Bellingham."

"Is that Washington or Worshington?" he gibes.

"Worshington," I reply.

I admire a guy who seems to lack a serious bone in his body. If he makes fun of dudes from the States (like me), no problem.

* * * * *

From the Comox ferry terminal at Little River, we drive south on Route 9A. I miss the turn off onto Route 9, but the Old Island Highway suits us just fine. Even at the slower pace on the two-lane road, we'll still make it to Chemainus in time for the ferry to Thetis Island. So why not go slow and enjoy the shoreline scenery?

At Parksville, we merge onto the four-lane Island Highway (Route 9) in order to bypass Nanaimo. We settle in at 90 klicks, while the thrum of *Mr. Kayak's* rooftop mounting straps resonate inside the Tempo.

"I hear you *Mr. Kayak*," I yell towards the roof.

"He's telling you to slow down," says Margy.

When those straps resonate, you know you're approaching the kayak's speed limit.

We start down a steep hill. The oncoming traffic winds up towards us is a nearly continuous line of RVs.

"Tourons," I say to Margy.

"Seems like so many," she replies. "Maybe it's just because we don't see this much traffic in Powell River."

She's right. You forget how busy the big highways are when you are sheltered by the peace and quiet of Powell River. I wouldn't trade it for anything.

* * * * *

The ferry to Thetis Island is barge-like, carrying three lines of cars. Vehicles are packed so tightly that mirrors must be folded inward during loading. Once aboard, there is no place to sit, but no one seems to mind. It's a gorgeous day, and everyone crowds to the front deck to watch the passing scenery; even the locals.

From the Thetis ferry terminal, we drive to Sunrise Point. We're the only ones launching a kayak at the moment, so we drive right down to the beach and take advantage of the peaceful lack of traffic. We offload *Mr. Kayak* and deposit our gear on the shore. Then I drive the Tempo back up the hill to the parking area. Meanwhile Margy organizes our overnight supplies and begins to stow them in the three watertight compartments.

"Big kayak," says a man lounging in a canvas lawn chair on the shore.

"It's got a third seat in the middle, for a child. Or a dog," I reply.

As we chat with the man, we realize he has a friend we know in Powell River, another example how small the world is on the BC coast. This seems to happen all of the time in this region; never in Los Angeles.

The man and his wife are on the beach today, absorbing the warm sun. They are visitors from nearby Comox, and are interested in our plans for camping overnight. They are surprised at the amount of gear we plan to load into the kayak, so I show them the large storage compartments and describe the route we plan to take. As Margy and I expound on our camping plans, we feel like sporty adventurers rather than the occasional kayakers we really are.

* * * * *

Finally, *Mr. Kayak* is in the water. Now the tough part – getting aboard. I hold the kayak in shallow water, while Margy steps into the front cockpit. She catches her foot on the rail and falls forward at an awkward angle. *Splash* – she's in the water. We are just beginning our journey, and already one of us has fallen into the ocean. Of course, the couple from Comox is still watching intently. Maybe we aren't experienced adventurers after all.

"I bet you don't think we know what we're doing," I yell back to them.

"Those things happen," yells the man. "Is she okay?"

"Sure!" I answer for Margy. "We handle things safely. We're just a bit clumsy."

Margy and I are both aboard now. I take a few moments in the aft cockpit to adjust my foot pedals, since I'll be steering with the rudder. We paddle out from the beach only a few metres, and pause there while I wrestle with the cable that deploys the rudder. At first the line seems jammed. Then the rudder plops down with a solid thud. We're off!

I push on the rudder pedals to point the bow towards the north end of Reid Island. This first stretch of open water will be one of the longest of the three-day trip. It's not a major obstacle, but it takes a lot of effort to paddle across the channel. If we had not started from Thetis Island, even more open water would need to be crossed.

Rounding the north end of Reid Island, Porlier Pass is finally in sight between Valdes and Galiano Island. The provincial park at the tip of Galiano Island should be a scenic camping spot, although the tide tables indicate that the water in the channel is running strong at the moment. I know Margy is apprehensive about tidal rapids, still recovering from Dodds Narrows, where she received her first taste of strong currents. The maximum velocity at Porlier Pass is nothing compared to Dodds Narrows.

"Do you think Porlier Pass floods from this side or the other?" I ask.

It's a tough question to answer, since the pass runs almost precisely east to west. I carry tidal charts, downloaded from the Internet the previous day, but they fail to tell me which way the current is running on this flooding tide. If the flow is from the east, it will be difficult to make it through the pass until near sunset when slack tide occurs. On the other hand, if it's flooding from the west, we could go for it in a few hours when the current lessens a bit. We could even ride the rising tide right up to the campground.

"I don't know which way it floods, but I don't like it," admits Margy.

"Let's just take a look," I suggest.

"Careful, please," she replies.

As we approach the pass, I can tell Margy is getting nervous. I offer some reassurance.

"According to the tide tables, it's only four knots now," I say.

"I can hear it. Sounds like a locomotive."

I can hear it too, but it sounds more like a breeze in the trees.

"Let's get a little closer," I propose.

"You can see the whitecaps over there." Margy uses her paddle to point to the left, near the tip of Valdes Island. White water rapids are generally beyond the limits of this sea kayak, paddled by amateurs.

I maneuver towards the Valdes (north) side of the channel. If we don't proceed through Porlier Pass, we'll steer farther to the north, not wasting a lot of paddling energy. The shoreline of Valdes Island will lead us to our alternate camping spot at Blackberry Point.

The kayak reacts to the flooding current that begins to draw us eastward through the pass. It's now clear that Porlier Pass is flooding from west to east, and ahead of us are the standing waves of tidal rapids, a powerful part of nature that always amazes me. This current is probably too much for us to tackle, and slack tide is still several hours away. Even then, Margy may not feel comfortable.

"Okay, I've seen enough," I say. "Let's head towards Blackberry Point."

"More left rudder, please!"

Margy says it in a strained voice that indicates she is worried about being sucked into the rapids. As usual, she is strong in the face of crisis, but quick to admit her concern for the power of nature. When nature strikes particularly hard, we make a good pair: I tend to get in over my head; she knows when to sound a warning that often saves us.

I angle the bow more directly towards Valdes Island. In a few minutes the whitewater is out of sight around the point, and the sound of the rapids is gone.

It's a long way to Blackberry Point, and we haven't paddled a kayak for any length of time for almost a year. We're not in top paddling condition, but, fortunately, the sea is nearly calm. We paddle past sandstone caves carved into the Valdes shoreline, riding only a few feet from the cliffs. Wave-carved hollows in the rock look more like the work of humans than nature. Sandstone cliffs spiral in all directions, an awesome sight.

We go ashore on a gravel beach for a rest. When we're ready to leave after our brief stay, Margy climbs into the kayak smoothly this time. When I step aboard from the left side, I stumble entering the cockpit, and fall out the other side. I catch myself with my arm on the kayak's gunnel just before I splash headfirst into the water, but it's close. I'm usually pretty surefooted getting in and out of a kayak, but not this time. In fact, if I had caught my arm on the kayak at a slightly different angle, I could have been badly injured. During only two kayak entries today, we have both fallen out of the boat.

At Blackberry Point, there are no campers. A small runabout is beached 50 metres down the shore, where two men and a woman sit aboard their boat, drinking beer and awaiting the sunset. We pull *Mr. Kayak* above the high tide mark and tie him to a tree. Then we set up our tent on the bluff and watch the sun drop down towards Vancouver Island. A few minutes after sunset, the runabout starts its engine and departs, while we settle in for a peaceful night.

A minor low-pressure trough is scheduled to pass through the area in another day, although it may be a non-event. I plan to keep a close eye on this disturbance to assure we don't get caught in a developing storm. Before going to bed, I look for my radio, to tune in a weather report. But my radio is not in any of the kayak's storage compartments, and it's not just the radio that is missing. Packed with the radio are my toothbrush, reading glasses, a book, and a reading light. I feel lost without these items, which now apparently sit in the car at Sunrise Point on Thetis Island.

In the middle of the night, I step out of the tent to check the night sky. The Big Dipper rides low in the north (as low as it gets at this high latitude), and the waning gibbous moon is rising behind the trees to the east. To the west, the lights of Chemainus burn bright.

I look for meteors. The annual Perseids shower is two days past peak, but stray meteors are common during this astronomical event. In a period of five minutes, under less than optimal conditions (bright moon and high wispy clouds), I see two meteors. Both emerge directly from the northeast, in the constellation of Perseus. It's always reassuring to know that there are places left in this world where normal-magnitude meteors can be seen routinely, even in less than optimum conditions. Los Angeles has its assets, but naked-eye astronomy isn't one of them.

* * * * *

When I awake in the morning, Blackberry Point is being thumped by small waves. The plan for our departure is to parallel the shore, paddling south for a few kilometres and then across the channel to Thetis Island. We'll slip along the Thetis shoreline down to Sunrise Point. Since our car is almost on the way to our next overnight stop at Wallace Island, why not pick up my radio and the other forgotten items on the way?

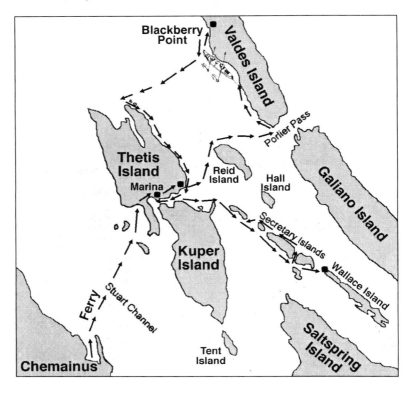

The planned route starts off well. After a short stretch of paddling along the shore, I aim the bow for the north end of Thetis. As we cross over the open water towards the island, waves quickly grow into two-foot whitecaps in swells rolling in from the northwest. Paddling becomes tough.

As we approach the north end of Thetis, I notice some rocky islets that may be worth exploring. In these heavier seas, it seems a long way that we still need to paddle.

"It's funny how far away land seems to be on a difficult crossing," says Margy. "Then suddenly – you're there."

She's right. That's exactly how it seems today. The islets were barely visible a few minutes ago, and seemed so far away. Now we are almost on top of them.

As we approach the islets, six cormorants take off from the outer islet and head our way. They drop low and join together in a loose formation, circling closely around us anti-clockwise. These long-necked birds appear to be scouts, sent out to see who we are and why we're coming. They make two complete circuits of our kayak in a formation that suddenly breaks down completely and then regroups quickly.

"It looks like a little Mitlenatch," I observe.

Birds flitter around the islets, rising and falling on the breeze. Their calls raise quite a ruckus.

We round the triangular navigation marker and pull inside the islets, to ride south on the wind. When we stop paddling, we are pushed by the wind. As we drift the entire length of the islets, we glide past a variety of birds perched on their nesting grounds. At the southern end, we pass only a few feet from two oystercatchers ("sea pies"), with their stark black bodies and bright red beaks. It's an enchanting close-up of nature, so common in coastal BC that you tend to take it for granted.

We paddle leisurely down the east side of Thetis, pushed by the wind, and come ashore at Sunrise Point. I walk up the hill to the parked car and retrieve the radio and my kit of personal items. Since we are so close, and it's nearly noon, we decide to stop for lunch at Telegraph Harbour Marina, which is located in the narrow channel that separates Thetis from Kuper Island. The two islands were once a single land mass with a narrow waist, until a channel was dug to allow boat traffic through at high tide. At low tide, it's navigable only by small boats that carefully follow the channel markers.

Now, even with low tide approaching, this route should not be a problem for our kayak if we follow the markers. Instead, I decide to take a shortcut to Clam Bay, which takes us across the lowest of the low water. We run aground on a shallow sandbar. After asking Margy to stay aboard, I step out into less than a foot of water; then I walk Margy and the kayak through a short stretch of very shallow water to rejoin the main channel.

At Telegraph Harbour, we pull *Mr. Kayak* out of the water near the cafe. A table at the door displays a variety of delicious looking pies. August is blackberry season in southern British Columbia, so besides our lunch, we select a blackberry pie to go.

There is another kind of pie on the menu – pizza. It should make an excellent evening meal at the Wallace Island campground, so we also order a medium cheese and pepperoni pizza to go. As we leave the cafe, walking back down to the kayak, we pass an older couple who are struggling a bit with the climb up the walkway from their boat.

"Good looking pies," says the man, as he sees what I am carrying.

"That's me, the pie man. Pizza and blackberry – what a combination."

"Works for me," laughs the man.

The pies will make a fine meal on Wallace Island, if they survive the journey.

Back at the kayak, I pull off the center and forward hatches and load the pies, wrapping them first in heavy plastic bags. The blackberry pie goes on top of the tent and air mattresses in the center compartment, a secure fit that will prevent damage. The pizza fits awkwardly inside the forward compartment. I smash the corners of the box, ramming it in, but it should endure the trip.

On the way out of the marina, we follow four triangular markers on the left that lead us through the deeper channel. We round Penelakut Spit, and find a bit of disturbed water at the tip. It flows in no particular direction, but the roiled current indicates tidal flow.

We follow along the west side of the Secretary Islands, where purple Pacific Starfish cling to the rocks, and arbutus trees grow out from the cliffs. At the end of the second island in the chain, Steller sea lions bask on the rocks with their pups. The youngsters are nearly fully grown now. As we approach them, they slide into the water. They bob a few feet from our passing kayak, giving us a close examination.

At the northern tip of Wallace Island, we go ashore in a cove where three other kayaks are already pulled up onto the beach. Since the tide is still rising, we take the extra time needed to haul our kayak onto a ledge above the high tide mark, but first we unload our camping gear to reduce the weight. The two pies have survived just fine.

That evening, Margy and I walk along the center-island trail for several kilometres. We find a cliff lookout where we can see the boat anchorage to the south at Canover Cove. Boat's to the south, kayaks to the north – it's a practical arrangement.

Dinner consists of pizza and blackberry pie in the luxury of a real campground, picnic table included. The pizza is good, and the berry pie is the best I've ever tasted. We devour most of the pizza and half of the pie, saving the rest for breakfast.

I tune in CBC radio, and hear a forecast that includes clouds overnight, with a mix of sun and clouds for tomorrow. The weak frontal disturbance is not going to spoil our trip.

* * * * *

The next morning, after finishing off what remains of both pies, we launch on a rising tide. It will provide a nice push on our return to Thetis Island. A southeast breeze propels us even more, as we drift along the west shore of the first Secretary island, with no need to paddle. We plan to deviate through the channel in between the islands to the other side of the Secretaries. As I compute it, the tidal flow should be towards the east in this narrow passage.

The current is bigger than expected. We glide past the rocks where we saw sea lions yesterday (now unoccupied), riding the two-knot flow towards the channel between the islands. We need to paddle only enough to stay headed in the right direction. On most of our kayak journeys, the trip home always seems to be into the wind and waves. But today we drift with the wind, with the waves at our backs, and we're further assisted by the favorable flow of the flooding tide.

Entering the channel between the islands, the current converges into a river-like flow. The passage winds majestically between the islands, with only an occasional dip of a paddle needed to stay on course. On the east side of the islands, the tailwind increases even more. I estimate our forward drift at three knots, perfect kayaking conditions. And to think we've found it on the typically demanding last leg of the trip.

This rugged side of these islands is in contrast to the weather-worn sandstone on the west side. I would have guessed that this side would be more battered by storms in strong southeasterly winds, but the slow but persistent wearing process of fair-weather westerly winds on the other side seems to win out.

As we drift along, I watch the boat traffic against the background of Galiano Island, to our right. It's late in the summer, so most of these boats are headed south. There is a bittersweet feeling when summer ends. But for Margy and me, with no kids going back to school and no demanding schedule to follow, we feel an immense sense of freedom. We sympathize with those going south, but we rejoice in not being among them. To be truthful, we laugh a bit about those who will soon be strapped to their office chairs in the city.

After passing Mowgli Island, we slip over to the west side again, riding what little remains of the tidal flow. We follow the shoreline of Norway Island, where I point the kayak towards a rocky beach between slabs of granite, perfect for beaching a kayak. In this rocky spot, we spend an hour swimming and exploring the tide pools.

Our last leg back to Sunrise Point is short, and soon we are ashore. We unload the kayak, reload the car, and drive to Telegraph Harbour. The ferry to Chemainus doesn't depart for over an hour; time enough for some more pie.

◊ ◊ ◊ ◊ ◊ ◊

Chapter 15

The Last Tourists

There's nothing wrong with cruising the straits of coastal British Columbia in July and August – except for the crowds. By city-folk standards, the density of boats is minimal even in the heart of summer, but my adopted coastal BC intolerance for crowds shows through.

An off-season trip in the Bayliner quickly reminds me of the difference between the tourist season and any other time of the year. In any season other than summer, anchoring in even the most popular spots is a private experience, so why not take advantage of it? The storm systems in the spring and autumn must be closely monitored, but there are plenty of weather windows if you keep a close (and patient) watch. Keeping your alternatives open also helps.

* * * * *

The Bayliner has been moored in Powell Lake for the entire summer. The stint in the lake has killed off the accumulation of saltwater critters clinging to the hull and the stern leg of the engine. As an added advantage, the boat has been available for occasional lake adventures, including two major motorcycle trips up the lake.

In August, while I am in Los Angeles, John moves the Bayliner back to Westview Harbour. It is ready to travel up the Strait of Georgia when I return in early September, but the weather doesn't immediately cooperate. A cold front moves through the area, producing stormy winds and a major downpour. As the skies clear, moderate northwest winds flow behind the front. The chuck settles down slowly; Sentry Shoal reports one-metre swells, which is close to my no-go limit for the Bayliner. The *Queen of Burnaby's* morning marine weather report, as it crosses from Comox to Powell River, indicates 35-knot winds and rough seas. Yet the conditions aloft are nearly ideal for flying. This prompts me to turn my attention to airplanes rather than boats. I ponder a flight to the Queen Charlotte Islands.

While I am isolated from both TV and the Internet at my cabin, John tracks the major weather systems for me on his television in town. With a little extrapolation, he is able to keep me informed about the expected conditions in the Queen Charlottes farther north. The entire summer has sped by without a single opportunity for the planned flight. There have been many clear days, but I need at least three of them in a row for the trip. Such a weather window is not unheard of, but it isn't wise to plan a flight to the Charlottes in a Piper Arrow, even during the summer, unless extended optimal weather seems assured.

I'm certified for instrument flying, but the Queen Charlottes are an area well known for violent storms. By all scales of judgment, this route is a remote one for a Piper Arrow. Fair weather is a necessity if I am to tackle this flight along the rugged northern BC coast. Once you leave Port Hardy, there are few airports along the way.

Similarly, the operating condition of the airplane must be perfect. This airplane has a good engine, but there is only one of them. Thus, on the first clear day after the last frontal surge of early September, I motor down the lake in the Campion with a bit of apprehension. The winds aloft are acceptable, and the Queen Charlottes sit within a cloudless high-pressure area. A rare forecast of three days of fair weather along the northern coast is difficult to ignore.

Upon arrival in town, I consult with John. The high-pressure system off the coast is huge. A dry offshore flow will dominate the weather picture along the entire coast for the rest of the week. But that's the forecast. Reality is not always in-tune with such predictions, particularly as summer transitions into fall. The BC coast is famous for its beautiful autumns, but clear spells on the north coast seldom last very long.

For me, the biggest lingering concern is the airplane. A minor oil leak that developed on the flight to Canada has become annoying. It's not significant enough to cancel my local flights, and I will have it looked into during the next oil change. The leak looks worse than it is – it doesn't take much of an oil leak to make a mess inside an airplane cowling. At 130 knots, the airflow through the engine compartment sweeps a few drops of oil all over the place. In this case, the oil is dripping onto the retracted nose landing gear, which is tucked away into the lower part of the cowling during flight. After landing, a mist of oil is visible on the nose strut. I've flown with leaks like this before without immediately tending to them. It's a reasonable decision when flying in areas with lots of nearby airports.

But as I think more about this leak (really only a slight seep), I imagine flying 600 kilometres north; then west across 100 kilometres of open water in Hecate Strait to Sandspit Airport. It's one of those concerns that starts small, but then begins to gnaw away at you. I try to decide *air* or *water* for the next day's journey, finally giving in to my concern about the oil seep. This rare weather window for flying is best ignored. There will be other days for the Charlottes.

* * * * *

The next morning dawns clear. From the condo's balcony, the chuck is smooth. There are no whitecaps visible anywhere, and the few sailboats out and about have their sails stowed; a good sign for powerboats.

The marine weather report indicates great conditions on the chuck, with a forecast to match. The high-pressure system is firmly anchored off the coast, and the havoc-causing trough has moved east and out of the area. The forecast is for northwest winds, light to moderate, the perfect indicator of prolonged fair weather.

Loading the boat for the first trip of the autumn season is always a chore. That's particularly true today, because our bicycles are on the packing list, along with provisions for several overnight trips up the strait.

Few boats are headed north in September. Most are already in their home ports after spending summer (or a few weeks) cruising the coast. Those that remain in the Strait of Georgia are typically headed south, homeward bound. I have been watching the southward stream of boats for the past week, imagining our Bayliner headed north against the flow. Going up the strait with few other boats competing for anchoring spots is a pleasant image.

I crank away at the starter after an obvious case of flooding the carburetor. Then I give it a rest and prepare for a flooded start. It looks like this trip may be over before it begins. But just as the battery seems to be losing its kick, the engine catches. *Vroom, vroom* – such a great sound!

* * * * *

Margy and I cruise northward past Dinner Rock on nearly flat sea conditions. Two Pacific white-sided dolphins play twenty metres to the left of our bow – a good sign.

The fuel dock at Lund is empty when we arrive, except for one sailboat at the end of the dock, probably parked there while the crew visits the bakery or hotel restaurant. During the summer, you would never see this. Instead, all boats would be hustled in and out of the fuel dock without having time for even a quick trip to shore.

The sign shows *Summer Hours*; farther below are *Winter Hours*. The summer hours are rubbed out, and the revised hours that are scratched in are illegible.

"Are you still on summer hours?" I ask the girl who hands me the fuel hose.

"Guess so," she replies. "We're open until 6 pm now."

"When does that change?" I ask.

We plan to make this a frequent fuel stop in the weeks ahead. It isn't even officially autumn yet.

"I've heard we're going to new hours soon, but I don't think it will be before the end of September." That's almost winter here.

Leaving Lund, I angle the boat outside of the Copeland Islands. We'll miss the best view of the islands from there, but we don't want to waste the remaining daylight. The outside passage of the islands will be quicker, since we won't have to slow to minimum wake speed, as we would within Thulin Passage. It's a common decision here – scenery versus time.

Our route takes us up Lewis Channel, along the east side of Cortes Island. Halfway up the passage, the wind changes; we leave the nearly calm conditions and encounter a moderate north wind. The airflow and accompanying small waves are now directly off our bow. It is not rough, but it is a change.

Slowly and for no apparent reason, the engine begins to wind down. At first, I think it is merely the throttle vibrating back towards idle, so I push it farther forward. The boat continues to mush and drops off-plane, although the engine does not seem to be at fault.

"We're losing power," says Margy. "Or is it the wind?"

My thoughts exactly. Usually a wind doesn't produce such a large change in forward progress. We continue to decelerate, although the engine sounds healthy. It's not a flameout; call it is a flame-down.

I give in to the situation and reduce the power to idle. We bob in choppy conditions in a narrow section of Lewis Channel, with three boats pushing south off our bow. We've seen few boats today, and now there are two cruisers and a large commercial fishing boat near us in a confined space. Our drifting course becomes a temporary obstacle for the other boats, but they adeptly maneuver around us.

I shift the engine into neutral and work the throttle forward and back – sounds fine. Then I try reversing the engine, and advance the power a bit.

"Maybe we've picked up some seaweed," I say. Sometimes reversing throws it off.

"Could it be the tide, mixed with the wind?" asks Margy. "It seems like we lost power gradually."

The wind is from the north, and the tide is ebbing from the south. Tides opposing the wind are sometimes challenging, although the tidal current here is puny, and the wind is no big deal.

When I power up again, all is fine. It's just one of those things you can't explain. Maybe it was seaweed; maybe not. In any case, the engine sounds fine, so why argue with success?

We round the northeast tip of Cortes Island and turn west through Sutil Channel towards our overnight destination, Von Donop Inlet. The inlet cuts a long sliver of sea into Cortes Island, so long that it almost connects with Squirrel Cove on the other side of the island.

On the way into the narrowest channel of Von Donop, there's one rock to watch out for, but it's clearly marked on the GPS and easily avoided.

"How many boats here?" quips Margy.

We're hoping there are none, but anything less than 20 in this large inlet will be bliss.

"I'll guess only two," I reply.

"I'll go with five," she predicts.

There are six. And that leaves a lot of space.

We tuck into the back of the bay, dropping anchor near the hiking path to Squirrel Cove that I've read about in a boating guidebook. According to our map of Cortes Island, the trail runs along the bay, with an access point on the east shoreline.

After anchoring, we launch *Mr. Bathtub*. I carry a small backpack for the hike to Squirrel Cove. Just in case Marilyn's Salmon Shack is

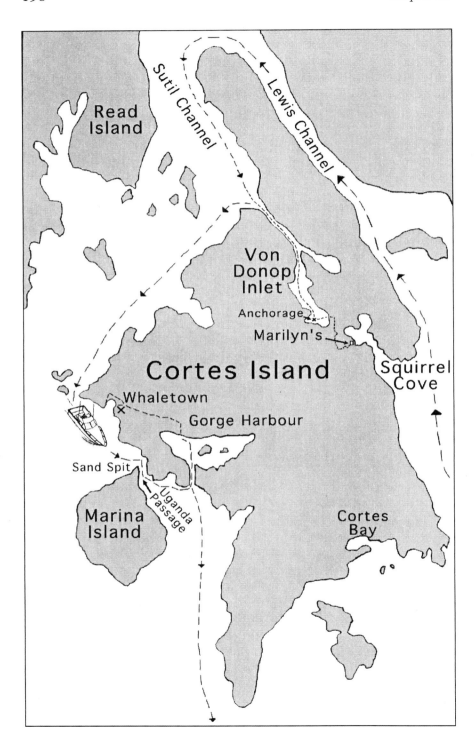

Read
Island

Sutil Channel

Lewis Channel

Von
Donop
Inlet

Anchorage

Marilyn's

Cortes Island

Squirrel
Cove

Whaletown

Gorge Harbour

Sand Spit

Uganda
Passage

Marina
Island

Cortes
Bay

open at the cove, I also have cash in the pack. Marilyn's hours of operation are far from reliable, but when this shed-like building is open, it's a real treat. Her blackberry pie is amazing.

Fully loaded with Margy, me, and the three-horsepower outboard motor, *Mr. Bathtub* cruises slowly. We avoid making any sudden moves that might upset the dinghy. I steer by carefully shifting my weight, while we scout the back of the bay for the beach trailhead. There are several promising locations, but nothing looks obvious. Eventually, I return to a prospective spot and run *Mr. Bathtub* up onto a course gravel beach, with the typical but uneasy scrunching sound of fiberglass against stone. We pull the dinghy above the high-tide mark and tie up to a hefty tree.

There is no trail here, but it is a fairly easy climb up a moderate slope. I'm certain the trail runs parallel to the shore, per the boating guidebook, so it is merely a matter of bushwhacking our way upward until we find it. After slogging through some switchbacks to avoid fallen logs, I find the trail and await Margy's slow-but-sure arrival.

The trail, built by the local First Nations, is of provincial park quality, well maintained and landscaped with logs placed at the sides. We start south, uphill along the trail. Judging by the steep gradient of the climb, there is no immediate danger Von Donop Inlet will ever be flooded through to Squirrel Cove, although a glance at a map might indicate otherwise. It is less than three kilometres between the two coves, separated by a small ridge that provides a geographic divide through the island. It's enough to keep these coves apart until the next biblical flood.

"It's uphill just a bit farther, and then all downhill," I proclaim, as we start to puff and pant on a long uphill stretch.

"I've heard that before," chides Margy.

And she has, because it is my way of trying to convince her (and me) that a climb is worth it, relief being right around the next bend. I tend to announce declarations of guaranteed downhill gradient as if I know what I'm talking about. In fact, it is only representative of my unrelenting optimism.

Signs along the way clearly show our progress, with countdown markers every half kilometre. We start near *2.5*, and by *1.0* we are still climbing.

"It's gotta start down soon," I say, but less convincingly this time.

"Or else it's a cliff at the Squirrel Cove end," says Margy.

Actually, we're doing okay, but it is amazing that there seems to be more uphill than downhill. Since both ends of this trail must be at sea level, that can't be true. Unless, of course, we're on the wrong trail.

This perception that we must be near the crest is like flying over a saddle in the clouds, climbing to avoid the turbulence and icing conditions inside the tops of the cumulus. Often it looks like the clouds have topped out, so a little more climb and a few more minutes of flight should lead to a downward glide with clear skies beyond. But sometimes the climb just continues.

Finally, near the 0.5 kilometre sign, the descent begins. Sea level is far below us.

"The hike back to the boat will be mostly downhill," I state.

Of course, with ocean on both ends of the trail, that is mathematically impossible.

A split in the trail is clearly marked by a post with three wooden arrows: *Squirrel Cove* straight ahead; *Von Donop* back where we came; and *Marilyn's Takeout* to the left. Marilyn has a knack for advertising in unique places.

The Squirrel Cove designated on the sign is the First Nations town (several kilometres south) rather than the nearby anchorage below us. Marilyn's Salmon Shack sits at the entrance to the anchorage, also called Squirrel Cove. I'm glad I've brought cash, just in case I have a chance to spend it.

We start down the path to Marilyn's. There's little chance she will be open. Even during the heart of summer, her hours are sporadic. But it would be a welcome treat to find Marilyn open for business at the end of this trail.

The path gets steeper, but Marilyn's signs keep hikers hopeful. *Marilyn's Takeout* arrows are planted every few hundred metres, even though there are no intersections where you could stray from the trail. Marilyn's signs are like highway billboards reminding you of an approaching *Eat Here* dining experience. Marilyn has a wise advertising manager.

"Marilyn needs to bring in the road crew to fix these potholes," I yell back to Margy, who is starting to fall behind in the descent.

"Needs work!" she replies.

The trail is now narrow and rocky. In fact, we are following a streambed that doubles as a trail as it descends to the cove below. It's dry now, but you'd need a white-water raft to get to Marilyn's in the spring. The stream's polished rocks make footing difficult in the steep descent, and Margy's pace slows dramatically in these conditions. No twisted ankles, please – it's three klicks back to the boat.

Soon I begin picking up the pace. It's getting dark in the woods, and Margy doesn't need to go the final few hundred metres to a closed salmon shack. I increase my stride, so that I can reach the closed shack and return uphill to meet her before she wastes her energy (and our time) on the final descent. We can then make it back at the boat by sunset. On the other hand, if Marilyn's is open, it will be unique to treat Margy to a slice of berry pie to-go in the middle of the forest.

I spot water through the trees. In a few more steps, the south end of the anchorage pops into view. Three boats are anchored in the south corner of the cove, an area that normally boasts twenty vessels in the middle of summer. I can see the edge of Marilyn's small dinghy dock, but her shack is still out of sight.

The final stretch crosses over a narrow wooden bridge. The shack jumps out of the trees. *Closed* hangs in the window.

I linger for a few minutes, remembering the atmosphere of this location during the summer. Probably no one has been here in weeks. Two empty wine bottles sit discarded along the edge of Marilyn's deck, remnants of an anonymous story of celebration; at least that's how I prefer to imagine it.

After a brief pause to say a final goodbye to summer, I begin the climb without berry pie. I'm surprised to meet Margy only a short distance up the path. Either she has hiked downhill faster than I expected, or I lost some moments in space-time on the deck at Marilyn's.

"No pie today," I announce.

"What a surprise."

Aware of the approaching darkness, Margy is quick to agree to start upward again with only my reports of the empty salmon shack below. She doesn't have to stand on Marilyn's deck to make her hike complete, and she understands the challenge of the dwindling sunlight.

* * * * *

The next morning, Margy and I lounge on the Bayliner's aft deck. The sun now rides in a graceful arc to the south, lower than in the heat of summer, but still wonderfully warm. In the shade of the boat's cabin, the warmth evaporates quickly. Low-angle shadows proclaim the advance of the seasons.

Motoring out of Von Donop Inlet, I point the Bayliner west along the top of Cortes Island. The anchorages at Quartz Bay and Carrington are empty, although they undoubtedly held a flotilla of boats only a few weeks ago.

Rounding the northwestern tip of the island, we cut south, with a passing glance into the bay at Whaletown. I see only an empty ferry dock and a few buildings, with a small pubic dock opposite the ferry terminal. I expect more at such a historic location, but I've learned that less on the surface is often better when viewed close-up. This small and unpopulated place should be easily explored on our bikes from our next destination, Gorge Harbour.

I prepare my chart for Uganda Passage. This should be an interesting challenge, even with the approaching high tide. Like many locations with underwater obstructions, this channel is more easily navigated at low tide, when the rising sea bottom is visible. Shark Spit sticks out from nearby Marina Island, stretching almost to the shoreline of Cortes. The spit is now almost invisible, although it's barely submerged.

A red navigation marker on a large rock sticks up prominently, but two shallow-water green markers blend into the sun's glare off our bow. Once the green markers are sighted, it's a clear but winding route along the Cortes shoreline. I drive slowly at near-idle. Visually, the area seems wide open all the way to Marina Island. But our charts don't lie – a major sand spit looms just underneath.

A gravelly fin-shaped beach, designated as "Fun Family Beach" in my boater's guidebook, lies adjacent to Shark Spit. The guide's map shows boats floating on picnic hooks along the beach. Today, under the mid-day September sun, the beach sits empty.

Exiting Uganda Passage, we come nose-to-nose with a small runabout that maneuvers around us on our port side. As the boat passes, it slows for entry to Uganda Passage. Like us, locals respect the presence of the unseen sand spit.

Now I prepare for entry to Gorge Harbour. As expected, it is both narrow and scenic. First Nations rock paintings adorn the cliff, just as described in my boating guide. I often look for such markings, but even those clearly noted in guidebooks are often difficult to see. This time, a bold white arrow points to the area where the drawings begin. Even with that aid, it takes my eyes a few moments to detect the paintings that blend into the granite cliff.

I keep to the left (cliff side) to avoid the charted rocks. Inside the harbour, an oyster farm dominates the center of the bay, and a government dock sits to the north side. The dock is full, and none are tourists, as evidenced by the classic workboat design of the vessels. At the nearby private marina, lines of docks stand nearly empty, so we turn in that direction. The marina will be a good spot to bring our bikes to shore.

Should we get gas here? It's best to never pass up an opportunity for gas, although we still have plenty to get us home.

Our decision is made for us. An attendant stands on the fuel dock, hose in hand, awaiting our arrival. I guess they're not selling much gas this week.

As we top off the tanks, I ask the attendant how today compares with Labor Day weekend, only a week ago.

"It's a lot different," he says. "This place was packed. Looks like you're still cruising though."

"Yes, but we're just out for a few days."

"From Campbell River?" he asks. Now there's a compliment I can handle. He thinks we're locals. We must look Canadian. Even with our BC flag on the bow and our local K-numbers on the side, most Canadians can see straight through us.

"No, Powell River," I answer proudly.

The attendant nods, and I smile. I'm not a tourist. I'm a local Canuck!

Recently, I was flattered when identified as a local by a young gas station attendant in Powell River. When we stopped at the station for a refill of our cabin's propane tank, I proudly hoisted the empty bottle over my head as I walked to the propane service nozzle.

"Tarzan," I said to the young attendant.

"Mighty strong," he laughed.

While I was in the office paying for the refill, the attendant loaded the tank into Margy's truck, chatting with her: "Doesn't he work for BC Hydro?" he asked. As a visitor from the States, I take that as a real compliment.

Before offloading our bikes, I open the boating guide to a page with a photo of Gorge Harbour. It's obviously summer in the photo, since boats line all of the docks, not an empty spot in sight. Today we are tied up to the best dock in the house, while the rest of the dock fingers sit empty except for two other powerboats like ours and a tin boat.

Margy and I push our bikes off the dock, up the ramp, and a bit farther uphill to level pavement near the general store. From here, it's a gentle climb to the main road, and then it's almost all uphill, about three kilometres worth. The hilly stretch ends at the turnoff for the Whaletown ferry.

That's how perceptions work when riding bikes. In reality, there are numerous downhill sections to provide momentum for the next uphill push, but all I seem to remember are those uphill grinds. Overall, Cortes Island is quite hilly, but most of the slopes can be biked, requiring only a little walking up the steeper sections.

From the ferry turnoff on the main road, a steep grade leads down to the dock. There's not much to see at the terminal, except for a family of four waiting for the Quadra Island ferry. Mom apprehensively watches her three sons as they practice their skateboard flips and reversals near the gate to the dock. She pretends an interest in the boys' skateboarding skills, but shows more worry than pride. It must be tough to be a mom on such a gorgeous island, with little to keep teenagers busy and out of trouble. On the other hand, an island is also one of the most marvelous learning environments in the world.

After the nice downhill ride to the ferry dock, we face another substantial walk as we push our bikes back up to the main road. At the intersection, nearly twenty signs point to every cafe and resort location on the island. Almost all are to the right, so we turn in that direction and head back along the way we came, until we come to a sign that marks the entrance to Whaletown.

It's another welcome downhill ride, winding into the tiny village past a church and small library. At the end of the road sits the general store (closed today, Sunday), post office, and government dock.

Standing on the pier, I look across the bay at the now departing ferry. A few boats bob on mooring buoys in the bay. It takes only a little contemplation to visualize whaling ships returning home to their rendering base at Whaletown. The year 1870 was the heyday of harpoons and tall ships. Today, my imagination is alive. I sense the excitement of arriving whale boats and hear the jubilant voices of proud sailors returning home.

There are no signs of summer tourists on the pier today. I sit on my bike, in this tranquil spot in the September sun, comfortably perched between the bustling Whaletown harbour of then and the historic island town of now.

◊ ◊ ◊ ◊ ◊ ◊

Chapter 16

Raise the Gemini

We all have our assignments on launch day, but we botch them. I'm supposed to retrieve a yellow towing rope from John's boat and bring it with me in the Campion. John is supposed to meet Valley Marine at the airport to supervise the removal of *Gemini* from the hangar and bring along extra gas for the Campion. Ed volunteers to bring heavy plastic bags to be filled with sand or rocks and used for ballast below decks.

As *Gemini* is trailered to Mowat Bay, John follows in his truck. Coming down the hill from the airport, a big wooden block tumbles off the tow truck, and John stops to retrieve it. He throws the metre-high block into the back of his truck and then diverts to the gas station. But when he gets there, he glances through his rear window – no gas can. So he leaves the gas station without the extra gas for the Campion. (Later, he finds the gas can hidden under the wooden block.)

Ed forgets the plastic bags. Meanwhile, at the Shinglemill, I try to untie the yellow rope from the transom of John's Hourston. I'm confronted by a John-knot, designed to remain tight. Not only is it a John-knot, the towing rope probably hasn't been untied for years. With weathering factors added to a John-knot, I face a nearly impossible task with the stiff rope. But I work at it, and work at it. Finally the knot comes loose in my now-blistered fingers. As I pull out of the Shinglemill in the Campion, headed for Mowat Bay, I'm running late.

As I round the log boom marking the end of Block Bay, I see *Gemini* riding on the trailer behind the tow vehicle, followed by John's truck, as they maneuver down the road to Mowat Bay. John's aborted stop at the gas station has allowed him to catch up with *Gemini*.

The Valley Marine driver adeptly backs the trailer down the launch ramp in a perfect arc. I tie up to the dock just as *Gemini* is released from the trailer. The boat splashes into the water and immediately rebounds upward like it's on a trampoline. It bobs next to the dock, held securely by a cargo strap John has attached to the bow ring.

"Floats like a cork," observes Ted of Valley Marine. "Too unstable to tow."

"We're only going to my cabin at Hole in the Wall," I counter. "We'll go slow."

As *Gemini* bobs up and down in the almost imperceptible ripples, John shakes his head in disappointment. We knew the boat would be light without an engine, but we weren't sure how high it would float. To John, this is discouraging, but I am exhilarated – *Gemini* is finally in the water!

"There's hardly anything in the water," says John. "Look at the bottom of the hull. The black paint should be almost completely submerged."

A one-foot ring of black paint remains above the water at the bow, a bit less at the stern. The electrical ground rod on the transom doesn't even touch the water.

"It doesn't ride as high in the rear as I expected," I say, trying to be optimistic. "Looks like the stuff we tore out up front almost makes up for the missing engine."

"Still way too high in the water," says John. "It'll tow really freaky. And it's top-heavy. Scary."

I hand John the yellow rope.

"Where'd you get this?" he asks. "That's not the rope you were supposed to bring."

"It was tied to your transom. I thought it was the one you wanted."

"No. I wanted the long yellow rope that's stored in my boat. I can't believe you got this one untied."

Neither can I.

"We'll need a lot more rope than this," says John. "At least a hundred feet."

I return to the Campion and find a variety of ropes. John ties them together with more John-knots, so no worries that they will come apart. We end up with 120 feet mix of ropes and straps strung together, connecting the Campion to *Gemini*.

"She bobs like a cork," says Ed, who has just arrived in his van. "You're not gonna try to tow it, are you?"

Thanks, we needed that, especially coming from a guy who knows boats. Of course, half the time I'm unable to tell whether Ed is kidding or not.

John and I hop aboard the Campion. John starts the engine and maneuvers the boat into position. Meanwhile, I toss a few loops of rope towards *Gemini*, being careful not to allow it to get tangled in the Campion's prop. John pulls forward a few metres to straighten the line between the two boats and applies a little power.

On first grab, *Gemini* heads to the right, reaches the full extent of the rope, and darts back to the left. As we pull away from the dock, *Gemini* swings in a series of giant S-turns. It's like towing a crooked log that refuses to straighten itself in the wake. *Gemini* rides like a kid's water toy, zigzagging back and forth behind the Campion. At each zag, the bobbing boat keels over precariously towards its side.

We stop and try shortening the rope, and *Gemini* rides better. Shorter still, and the boat weaves more violently from side to side. We finally settle on 60 feet of rope, putting up with *Gemini's* S-turns for the two-hour tow to Hole in the Wall. Fortunately, the lake is relatively calm, and we arrive at the dock behind Cabin Number 3 without any major problems. The major challenges of this project are now behind us. Not!

John and I tie *Gemini* snug against its fenders. This should provide the boat with improved stability until we can add ballast below the decks.

John is concerned with a small amount of water that has already entered the bilge. It's not enough to activate the bilge pump's float switch, but why is there any water here at all? Maybe water splashed over the transom during the tow, although that seems unlikely.

"Could be old water that didn't show up in the hangar because of the angle of the blocks," says John.

I know John; he doesn't believe this. But he shows little worry, so neither do I.

We sit on the front deck of Cabin Number 3, discussing how to add weight to the keel.

"Sand would work, but it will be a mess if it gets wet," says John. "Cement would be good, or maybe just rocks."

Rocks become our ballast-of-choice for the moment, although John is concerned about the rocks wearing against the inside of the hull. Hole in the Wall is a relatively calm spot, but we do get storms, and the wakes from passing boats could cause rock abrasion against the hull. But with adequate protection of the hull from movement of the rocks, it should work. For one thing, rocks are readily available at nearby Sandy Beach, and the tin boat sits ready to haul them. A bottom lining of rubber or mill felt, bagged rocks, or a combination of both, should take care of rubbing against the inside of the hull.

* * * * *

The next morning, I check the bilge, and observe an increased amount of water. I override the float switch to pump out three buckets of water. Water is definitely coming in somewhere, but it is (for now) an acceptable leak. The bilge pump is rated to handle up to 500 gallons per hour, and the skookum solar power system can keep it powered as much as necessary. But it is beginning to look like *Gemini* will need to come out of the water for repairs. That means another tow down the lake, to the airport hangar, and then back to Hole in the Wall – not a pleasant prospect.

Later in the afternoon, Margy and I visit Sandy Beach in the tin boat. We load rocks into eight small buckets, along with one large plastic bucket that we place in the center of the tin boat. Within an hour, we are on our way back to our cabin, plowing low in the water.

I call Rick on the satellite phone to discuss the situation regarding our leak. John has left on a trip in the Bayliner with a friend, but Rick is glad to assist with ideas. He concurs with my plan to load rocks in various areas of *Gemini*, in an attempt to isolate the location of the leak. I will load the stern first, hoping the leak will stop, indicating water is entering from the bow. If it is a bow leak, we might be able to pull the cork-like boat onto the dock at the cabin for "dry dock" repairs. Maybe a trip back down the lake can be avoided.

Margy and I bag the rocks and place them in the stern storage boxes John has designed for the ballast. After filling the wooden boxes, I estimate we have added 400 pounds to the rear of the boat. Now *Gemini* sits noticeably stern-low, although the boat still rides, overall, high in the water.

I stick my head down into the confining bilge pump hatch and look towards the bow. Using a flashlight, I find no obvious places where the boat is leaking, although water seems to be building fastest on the port side of the bilge. I've discussed ideas with Rick regarding how to determine the rate of leakage. I remove the bilge pump from its rear cavity and place it on the aft deck. Now any water that enters the bilge compartment will stay there so I can take an accurate measurement.

Every few hours I inspect the water level in the bilge. Yes, it is increasing. No, it is not yet a serious problem. I determine the approximate amount of leakage by reinserting the bilge pump every few hours to extract the water into a bucket. My calculations indicate that *Gemini* is taking on water at a rate of about a gallon per hour.

Overnight, the boat's rate of leakage remains the same. I'm still hoping for a bow leak, so the best way to test for this is to raise the bow even farther out of the water. More rocks in the stern will help us reach that goal.

Margy and I return to Sandy Beach, where we load our buckets with another 400 pounds of rocks. Back at the cabin, we put the rocks into double-strength garbage bags, which will make it a lot easier to remove them from *Gemini* if we need to, and we stack the bags in the stern. By the end of the day, the transom rides even lower in the water. I adjust the dock lines to accommodate the new tilt of the boat and step back onto *Gemini's* aft deck for a final inspection of our work.

I'm greeted by a distinct gurgling sound – a disturbing flow of water, like a faucet running at low volume. It's coming from below the aft deck!

I lie on my stomach, stick my head into the bilge, and shine my flashlight toward the bow. An arc of water gushes up from the port side, about a metre forward of the bilge pump. Water spurts upward like a fountain, just to the left of the keel. In fact, in size and volume, it looks exactly like a drinking fountain, and it's rapidly filling the bilge.

"We need to get the rocks out!" I yell to Margy.

We drag buckets and bags of rocks across the aft deck, lift them over the gunnel, and dump them onto the dock. Within 15 minutes we are finished, but the gurgling continues unabated. The boat is back to its nearly-level (cork-bobbing) condition, but water continues to pour in.

To put it in basic terms, we have sprung a leak. Either our original seep has become a full-fledged leak, or it's a new one.

I quickly consider our options. I could attack the boat's aft deck (newly floored and painted) with my chain saw, to provide access to the leak. But how will I stop a major leak even if I reach it?

Margy and I discuss towing *Gemini* to a beach where it can sink into shallow water. That would prevent losing the entire boat, a possibility that has now reared its ugly head. Sandy Beach is my first thought, but it is in-line with waves that batter the shore from the south. The back of the bay behind John's Cabin Number 2 would be a lot calmer and a lot closer. We could use the tin boat to tow *Gemini* to the back of the bay in a matter of minutes, if it becomes necessary. As light as this boat is, we consider taking it ashore stern-first. That should reduce the leak's rate of flow and prevent further flooding of the entire structure.

We also discuss putting rocks back into the bow to try raising the stern. (Yes, we're getting whacky at this point.) But for now, the bilge pump is keeping up with the leak, automatically activating every hour as the water builds up in the stern. Leave bad-enough alone.

In fact, adding rocks again is eventually what we do in our attempt to increase the weight in the bow and raise the stern higher. So after 800 pounds of rocks have already been loaded into the boat and then removed, they now go back in again. But even after loading rocks into the bow, the gushing water continues to pour in. It's definite – we have sprung a major leak. I probably should be panicking, but instead I find myself visualizing a cartoon that only Ed could do justice to: a boat is sinking, with a leak spouting skyward in a high arc, while the captain plows full speed ahead. As the happy-go-lucky sailor says in my favorite boat movie, *Captain Ron*: "Hey, it's a boat. You have to expect a little water."

Margy and I attempt to raise the left side of the stern higher by sitting on the starboard rail. Maybe we can get the leak out of the water. The stern's port side bobs up, and there is a loud *Clunk!* I step out onto the dock to find the boat's left rear corner resting precariously up on the dock, raised onto the wooden ledge by the weight of our bodies on the starboard side. It's a clear hint – we may be able to lift this cork-like boat farther onto the dock.

And we do. If nothing else, the leak is not as far below the surface of the water now, so the pressure pushing the water into the boat is reduced. We use fenders and ropes to protect the edge of the stern and keep it braced tightly against the dock. We move rocks *again* (all 800 pounds!) to the boat's starboard side to keep the dockside edge as far out of the water as possible. There is little more to do except hope the leak doesn't get any larger. And so we wait for things to stabilize.

During the night, the wind begins to blow, but *Gemini* holds her position. The bilge pump's float switch activates every hour, pumping out water for six minutes at a time. If the rating of the pump is really correct (500 gallons per hour), six minutes equates to 50 gallons per hour! Throughout the night, I check the boat every few hours to assure myself that the bilge pump has not failed.

In the morning, I use a bucket-catching-method to verify that the rate is 30 gallons per hour. It's a serious leak, but still within the capacity of the bilge pump.

In the morning, I call Rick on the satellite phone to report the patient is in serious but stable condition. We discuss methods for forming a temporary plug, but it would be risky, maybe making the leak worse. Right now, the bilge pump is keeping up with the leak. Any physical probing of the leak's source to insert a plug could change things fast. I elect to wait for John's return to further assess the situation and decide how to handle the repairs. (Welcome home, John! *Gemini* is sinking!)

* * * * *

John's trip in the Bayliner began as a three-day voyage, but has extended to six days, and I have no way to contact him. So I babysit *Gemini* longer than expected. It's a fine excuse to spend extended time on the float during a period of perfect end-of-summer weather. Like Old Faithful, *Gemini* spurts water out her bilge pump every hour.

* * * * *

The troops arrive in force on Saturday morning. The Hourston pulls in with John and Bro aboard. They carry a boatload of equipment: a turfer (winch) and cable, a large pad of mill felt, two power saws, a grinder, and tools galore. Rick and Monique follow a few minutes later in Rick's new 16-foot aluminum boat. This boat suits Rick's personality perfectly – a sleek design with a hefty center console and a wave-bashing 35-horsepower outboard.

As soon as he is out of his boat, John pokes his head inside *Gemini's* bilge to inspect the fountain-like leak. Rick is in the water a few minutes later, plunging under the stern, wearing my bright pink facemask (minus snorkel). The leak is quickly located, analyzed, and temporarily plugged with a bolt that Rick pushes in from below. The flow continues, but now it slows to a mere seep, slow enough to allow us to calmly discuss permanent repairs.

The dry dock John selects, the muddy-shore behind Cabin Number 2, is far from dry. First, John drills holes in the transom to attach two U-bolts that will be used to hoist *Gemini* onto shore, stern first.

We load up the tin boat with the tools we'll need at the dry dock, including my gas generator for the power saws and grinder, the pad of mill felt, and three newly commissioned marine salvage engineers: John, Margy, and Bro.

I ride aboard *Gemini*, as the tin boat tows us across the Hole. I prop the bilge pump's float switch "on" with a stick to try to pump out most of the water in the keel. During the slow tow, the bow comes up high enough for the pump to suck out even more water from the bilge. The boat's cabin is now bare, with the carpet removed in case the soon-to-be low bow causes the floor to flood.

I use an oar to guide the boat through the narrow log boom entrance at Cabin Number 2. In the back of the bay, we use ropes to turn *Gemini* around and point the stern towards a massive fir tree that will be used as the attachment location for the winch. The pad of mill felt is laid out on the shoreline to minimize hull damage.

John sets up the winch system by tying a rope around the fir tree, attaching the turfer, and connecting *Gemini's* stern ropes (from the new U-bolts) to the other end of the turfer. We're ready to winch the boat onto the muddy shore.

Gemini is hoisted ashore with barely a groan from her hull. Gradually, the stern rises onto the shore, until the leaking area of the hull is in shallow mud.

John hops aboard *Gemini* with his tools, and marks off where he will cut into the aft deck with his skill saw. Margy uses the tin boat to return to Cabin Number 3 for additional tools, while Bro hunts frogs in the shallow water. I sit on a log, waiting for John to call for needed tools and materials. John is used to working by himself, but he always seems to enjoy the minimal luxury I provide by assisting, even if it is only to hand him tools when needed. When, John is ready for the generator for his skill saw, he calls to me, and I fire it up for him.

Once John has the aft deck cut open, he finds water still oozing up into the keel from the mud below. To hoist *Gemini* farther ashore would make it difficult to get the boat back into the water when the repairs are complete, so John decides to roll the boat over onto its side.

We attach the turfer to a stump on the right side of the boat. Using a rope attached to the stern's left rail, we roll the hull gradually up and onto its starboard side. John operates the winch, while I push from the boat's left side. As *Gemini* inches upward in a slow roll, Margy slips boards below the transom. In a few minutes, the leak is fully out of the water, ready for drying overnight. Tomorrow, John will add a fiberglass patch.

* * * * *

The following morning, John and Bro arrive in the Hourston with more tools and fiberglass patching material. I assist (tool handler), as John patches the leak and Bro, as usual, hunts for frogs. We let the fiberglass patch dry for the rest of the day.

Just before evening, we attach a rope to *Gemini's* bow, remove the winch, and prepare to pull the boat from the shore. Aboard the Campion, John takes up the slack in the 100-foot tow-line, while I float nearby in the tin boat. Margy monitors the stern from shore.

On the first tug, *Gemini* breaks loose from the mud and the wooden supports under the stern. The boat shoots forward, heading straight for the biggest stump in John's bay.

"Get it!" yells John. The slack in the tow-line provides him with no control over *Gemini* as it bolts forward. But the tin boat's small Evinrude hesitates as I apply power and dies. By the time I restart the engine, it's too late. *Whack!* goes the bow against the stump, a direct hit.

But no damage is done. *Gemini* is just exercising her new-found freedom.

I pick up Margy from shore. She takes command of the tin boat and pulls abeam *Gemini* where I can grab the aft rail and climb aboard. John shortens the towing line and deftly maneuvers out of the bay. *Gemini* is going home.

* * * * *

Overnight I monitor the newly plugged leak with the bilge pump turned off, crawling out of bed twice in the middle of the night to make sure all is well. In the morning, I remove only three litres of residual water from the bilge. By the end of the day, the bilge compartment remains dry. Finally, the boat is no longer leaking.

Now it's time to add rocks once again (last time!). I now have access to the keel through the new hatch John has cut to repair the leak, so I line the center trough with mill felt, transfer some of the rocks to heavy plastic bags, and stack the central well with the ballast needed to provide stability. Rocks are added below the cabin floor too, and larger decorative stones are displayed inside my new "office." The boat has regained the weight and balance for which it was originally designed, despite the missing engine and gutted interior.

I end the day by relaxing on the bench seat on *Gemini's* aft deck, listening to a radio powered by the boat's solar electrical system. This boat has come a long way. She isn't a writer's retreat quite yet, but *Gemini* sits proudly in her berth behind Cabin Number 3, awaiting assignments from the publisher.

◊ ◊ ◊ ◊ ◊ ◊ ◊

Epilogue

Straits and Inlets

Halcyon Days is the perfect boat. At 24 feet, most would consider this Bayliner inadequate for voyages on the Strait of Georgia. Then again, when John picked this boat out for me, it was supposed to be a transitional boat, a recreational craft that would serve as my introduction to the chuck. It was to be used carefully and only in the best of weather.

John constantly reminds me the Bayliner has an underpowered gasoline engine, and I need a diesel. And the dinghy, *Mr. Bathtub*, is notorious for instability. *Halcyon Days* is destined to be replaced someday by a bigger boat to carry me to majestic inlets farther north.

This boat has served its purpose well. I've watched the weather and limited my voyages to nearby destinations. The Bayliner has carried me securely up and down the Strait of Georgia, with few problems. In fair seas, I could journey even farther. I dream of the inlets to the north: Bute, Knight, and even Kingcome.

Thus, the problem – *Halcyon Days* is the perfect boat. Not perfect in size, although I love her compact dimensions. She is a joy to drive and contains everything I need. Docking this boat, even for an amateur like me, is a delight. I doubt I could ever say that about a larger vessel. How can I give up a perfect boat?

Four years have passed, and the Bayliner is still a transitional boat. I may never move up to anything larger. If I don't, what about Knight Inlet? I guess I'll just have to watch the weather. After all, *Up the Strait* is a book that is limited by its own geography. *Up the Inlet*, a writing project already enticing me, will push farther north. *Halcyon Days* is the perfect boat for the challenge.

◊ ◊ ◊ ◊ ◊ ◊ ◊

About the Author

Author with *Mr. Bathtub* at North Thormanby Island, Strait of Georgia

From 1980 to 2005, Wayne Lutz held the position of Chairman of the Aeronautics Department at Mount San Antonio College in Los Angeles. He led the college's Flying Team to championships as Top Community College in the United States seven times. He has also served 20 years as a U.S. Air Force C-130 aircraft maintenance officer. His educational background includes a B.S. degree in physics from the University of Buffalo and an M.S. in systems management from the University of Southern California.

The author is a flight instructor with 7000 hours of flying experience. For the past three decades, he has spent summers in Canada, exploring remote regions in his Piper Arrow, camping next to his airplane. The author resides in a floating cabin on Canada's Powell Lake and in a city-folk condo in Los Angeles. His writing genres include regional Canadian publications and science fiction. The author's next book, *Up the Airway*, is scheduled for release in early 2008.

Up the Lake
Up the Main
Up the Winter Trail
Up the Strait
Up the Airway

Order books and Photo CDs at:
www.PowellRiverBooks.com

Free Audio Chapters for the first 5 books
in this series are now available at the
Powell River Books web site

Reader's can email the author at:
wlutz@mtsac.edu
Blog — PowellRiverBooks.blogspot.com

Up the Strait is the fourth in a series of
volumes focusing on the unique places and
memorable people of coastal British Columbia

Future books in this series, currently in-work:

Up the Airway
More Up the Main
Up the Inlet

To check the progress of these books, or to register for notification of publication dates, visit www.PowellRiverBooks.com